ANGLO SAXON NORTHUMBRIA

PREFACE TO THE ORIGINAL EDITION, 1973

In proceeding from Roman Britain to Anglo Saxon England, a writer is immediately faced with intractable material. It is fragmentary, limited, scattered and there is a lack of order, clarity and preciseness. I have tried to piece together a story from documentary evidence and archaeological remains. Like Bede, I owe a good deal to the conversation of others and lectures, in particular to Mr. Brian Hope Taylor and Professor Rosemary Cramp. I have to thank Mr. Richard Bailey of Newcastle University for reading through my work originally and offering helpful advice. Dr. David Smith of the Museum of Antiquities has helped with the illustrations and my wife, again, has done the typing. **T.H. Rowland.**

PUBLISHERS NOTE TO NEW EDITION, 1994

The author has considerably revised and extended his original work to produce this new edition, which has been designed and reset in Times pt. 10 by Sandhill Press.

ANGLO SAXON NORTHUMBRIA

by

T.H. ROWLAND

SANDHILL PRESS

First published by F. Graham in 1973.
This revised and extended edition published in 1994.

© T.H. Rowland.

Sandhill Press Ltd.,
17 Castle Street,
Warkworth, Morpeth,
Northumberland, NE65 0UW.

ISBN 0 946098 34 4

Cover photograph : *Statue of St. Aidan, Lindisfarne.*
© Sandhill Press.

Printed by Martins the Printers Ltd.
Berwick upon Tweed

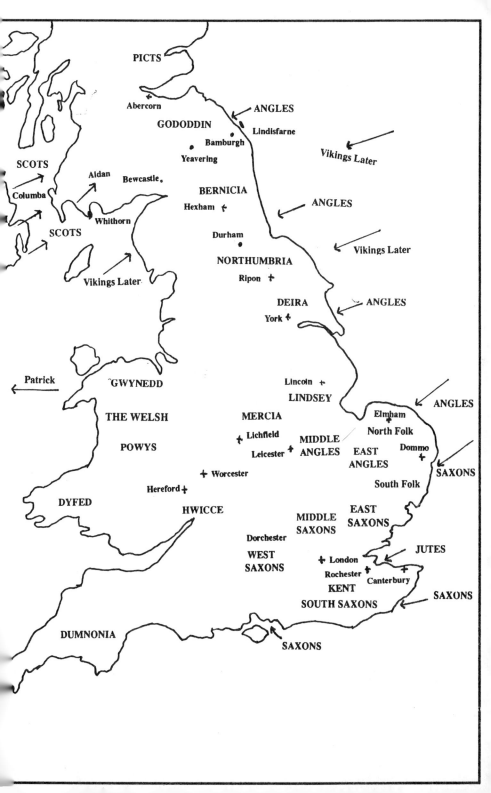

CONTENTS

PHOTOGRAPHS

Note: Illustrations of crosses from 'Northumbrian Crosses of the Pre-Norman Age' by G.W. Collingwood, pub. 1927.

ANGLO SAXON NORTHUMBRIA

Britain had been united by the Romans, but for most of their rule what we call Northumberland was beyond the frontier of the province, though closely connected with it. When the Romans withdrew, Anglo-Saxon settlers came and divided the land into many small kingdoms. Roman towns were neglected and decayed. A Saxon poet describes what many must have seen in a poem entitled 'The Ruin', which is a description of a deserted Roman city, written on two leaves badly scarred by fire:

Well-wrought this wall: Wierds broke it.
The stronghold burst....

Snapped rooftrees, towers fallen,
the work of the Giants, the stonesmiths,
mouldreth.
>   *Rime scoureth gatetowers*
>   *rime on mortar.*

Shattered the showershields, roofs ruined,
age underate them.
>   *And the wielders and wrights?*
Earthgrip holds them - gone, long gone,
fast in gravesgrasp while fifty fathers
and sons have passed.
>   *Wall stood,*
grey lichen, red stone, kings fell often,
stood under storms, high arch crashed -
stands yet the wallstone, hacked by weapons,
by files grim-ground...
...shone the old skilled work
...sank to loam-crust.

Mood quickened mind, and a man of wit,
cunning in rings, bound bravely the wallbase
with iron, a wonder.
>   *Bright were the buildings, halls where springs ran,*
high, horngabled, much throng-noise;
these many mead-halls men filled
with loud cheerfulness: Wierd changed that.

Came days of pestilence, on all sides men fell dead,
dead fetched off the flower of the people;
where they stood to fight, waste places
and on the acropolis, ruins.
                    Hosts who would build again
shrank to the earth. Therefore are these courts dreary and that red arch
twisteth tiles,
wryeth from roof-ridge, reacheth groundwards...
Broken blocks...

            There once many a man
mood-glad, goldbright, of gleams garnished,
flushed with wine-pride, flashing war-gear,
gazed on wrought gemstones, on gold, on silver,
on wealth held and hoarded, on light-filled amber,
on this bright burg of broad dominion.

Stood stone houses; wide streams welled
hot from source, and a wall all caught
in its bright bosom, that the baths were
hot at hall's hearth; that was fitting...

Thence hot streams, loosed, ran over hoar stone
unto the ring-tank...
... It is a kingly thing
...city...

(taken from 'The Earliest English Poems' trans. by Michael Alexander. Penguin.)

But it was not the end, for Christian churches were established on or near Roman sites. In Northumberland those at Corbridge, Bywell, Ovingham and Hexham were built of Roman stone, taken from the forts Chesters or Corbridge. Roman columns and arches were re-erected and the head of all the churches was the Bishop of Rome, no longer the Emperor. Anglo Saxon history is essentially the history of Christianity, and the Venerable Bede has been described as the 'Father of English History'. He provided the chronology, dating events from the time of the Birth of Christ. Today we use the Roman names of months and Anglo Saxon gods and goddesses give us their days of the week.

Bede tells us that after the departure of the Romans, invading tribes were Angles, Jutes and Saxons from North Germany and Denmark. The Saxons settled in kingdoms known as Essex (East Saxons), Sussex (South Saxons) and Wessex (West Saxons). The Jutes settled in Kent and Angles in East Anglia, divided between

Northfolk and Southfolk. Angles also settled in the whole area north of the river Humber and a kingdom emerged called Northumbria. Pope Gregory saw a number of fair-haired 'Angles' in the slave market at Rome, and said that they should be converted as 'Angels' to Christianity. St Augustine came to England (the land of the Angles) in 597 A.D. for the purpose of converting the people to the worship of Christ. Canterbury, formerly a Roman town, became his headquarters and a Roman Christian church was used. Recent excavations at the Cathedral, have revealed the remains of a very large Saxon building that was burnt in 1067.

In the north, Hadrian's Wall is the outstanding monument of the Romans, and Durham Cathedral that of the Normans. Anglo Saxon remains are much less impressive, but reveal a people more progressive than sometimes supposed. A great deal of evidence comes from cemeteries and burials – not only the grave goods, but information about the status, age and sex of the dead. Much plunder from England reposes in Scandinavian museums with ships of the time that combined trade with piracy. The articles that were looted show great skill in craftsmanship and indicate owners of some status.

The population of England was greater than supposed and a larger proportion of Britons survived. There is archaeological evidence that Britons and Saxons inhabited the same sites, churches replacing pagan temples. For example at Yeavering there is evidence of both. A typical prehistoric enclosure used as a gathering place for marketing, tax collecting, religious assemblies, feasting and 'moots' political assemblies where kings met their thegns. There were discussions on war, peace and religion, and the king bestowed awards on his leading men for their services. There was much eating and drinking, telling of stories and music from the bards.

Northumbria became one of the largest Anglo Saxon kingdoms, stretching at one time from the Humber to the Firth of Forth and including the whole of North Britain. It was created in the early years of the seventh century by the union of two kingdoms, the northerly Bernicia (of the mountains) and the southerly Deira (of the waters) – thus containing 'the people living to the North of the Humber'. Unlike the names of kingdoms in South England, these are British. It indicates an amalgamation of peoples in this wide area. The cemeteries in the North of England do not indicate occupation of the same density as in the South. But there is evidence of early settlement in York itself and the East Riding where Romano-British and Anglo-Saxon occupation merge. The explanation may well be the employment of German mercenaries both in late Roman times and after. Out of these settlements strengthened by other invaders grew the kingdom of Deira. Aelle is their first recorded king, and it was slaves from this area that were seen by Gregory in the Roman slave market.

Anglo-Saxon Settlements

Between the departure of the Romans and the emergence of the Anglo-Saxon kingdoms there elapses a period of two hundred years – a period of great activity and political change. One of the early historians, Gildas, has been regarded in the light of an Old Testament prophet indicating that disaster for the Britons was the result of their sins and of summoning to their assistance heathens, instead of fighting for themselves. He also gives wrong dates to the Roman Walls – dating construction to about the end of the fourth century. He adds that when the Romans refused a final appeal for help, some Britons gave up, but others fought bravely and drove back the enemy, thus gaining a period of peace and prosperity. But at a later date, a proud tyrant called in the help of the Saxons against the Picts and Scots. At first this was successful, but in due course the mercenaries turned against their paymaster, and fighting followed. Once again the Britons under Ambrosius Aurelianus defeated the Saxons, many of whom recrossed to the continent. (There is evidence of settlement in N.W. France.) Apart from dating of the Walls, much of this is acceptable, and Bede using Gildas goes even further, and gives the name of the tyrant as Vortigern, and the date of settlement 449 A.D. Nennius has it that relatives of Hengest, who helped Vortigern, settled in lands as far as the borders of the Picts. These leaders were named Octha and Ebissa, and it would seem that there was some settlement in N.E. England or S.E. Scotland about this time (449).

In North Britain three powerful kingdoms had been established. On the western side between the Walls of Hadrian and Antoninus was the kingdom of Strathclyde with its capital at Dumbarton. The other to the West was Reged which had its capital at Carlisle and, thirdly, to the East was Manau Gododdin (of the Votadini). This kingdom had a shorter life since it was exposed to Anglian attacks. Again about the date 450 many of its people with their ruler Cunedda transferred to North Wales to counter the threat of the Scots from Ireland. They were successful, but the kingdom of Manau was weakened, and, although a son of Cunedda stayed, it was difficult to resist the attacks of the Picts. Saxon mercenaries were employed against them, and were able to gain a footing in Yorkshire. This in course of time developed into the kingdom of Deira. An offshoot of this perhaps secured a footing at Bamburgh, and so the kingdom of Bernicia was born.

Information about the Anglo-Saxons is obtained from the writings mentioned of Gildas, Nennius and in particular Bede's 'Ecclesiastical History', which was completed in 731. Bede, who spent much of his life at Jarrow, is justly regarded as a great historian. First he gives a general description of the country, and then proceeds with its history from Roman times. He mentions the Wall – *"Severus built a rampart and ditch of this type from sea to sea and fortified it with a series of towers... The Romans had occupied the country South of the earthwork which, as I have said, Severus built across the island, as cities, temples, bridges and paved roads bear witness to this day..."* This is an interesting reminder of what archaeological remains were visible in the eighth century. He mentions the development of Christianity, and in 449 the coming of the Angles. The three races came from North Germany, the Jutes probably from areas closer to the Rhine than he thought. The Jutes settled in Kent; the Saxons in Essex, Middlesex, Sussex and Wessex; the Angles in E. Anglia, Mercia and Northumbria. He complains of the Britons *"that they never preached the Faith to the Saxons who dwelt among them."* This indicates that there was some intermingling of races, and not wholesale slaughter by the invaders.

The Anglo-Saxon Chronicle, although of later date, records the Anglo-Saxon invasions and settlements in more detail. Many traditions and genealogies were handed on, and eventually written. The names of the leaders and early kings are recorded. This, together with discoveries like the Sutton Hoo Burial and poems, such as the heroic deeds of Beowulf, enable us to piece together a picture of the life of the Anglo-Saxons. Bede includes information that is not contained in the Anglo-Saxon Chronicle; he obviously had access to material that has disappeared.

Among the Anglo-Saxons there were strong feelings of kinship and of similar racial origin. This feeling remained after their settlement in England as shown by the fact that English missionaries were ready to go back to Germany to try and convert the Germanic tribes to Christianity, a religion they had acquired in their new country.

The Saxon settlement of England took a very considerable time – it is 600 A.D. before the kingdoms emerge distinctly. The coming of Christianity to Kent provides us with our first written English laws. Till this time 'dooms' depended on oral tradition. In government, although Anglo-Saxon leaders claimed direct descent from Woden, a great deal depended on discussion in the assembly or 'moot'. A king was expected to listen to 'rede' or advice, and he who would not listen was foredoomed to failure and defeat.

The Anglo-Saxon Chronicle presents them, the leaders, arriving with two or three ships, seeking plunder or preparing to stay as the situation suited them. The place would be named after the leader, and so it is possible to trace settlements in this way – by names or by cemeteries, because the buildings which were of timber, did not endure.

For 547 the Anglo-Saxon Chronicle enters:

"In this year Ida from whom the royal family of the Northumbrians took its rise, succeeded to the kingdom... And he reigned 12 years and he built Bamburgh, which was first enclosed with a hedge (palisade) and afterwards with a wall (rampart)."

The invaders, having secured island or headland bases, moved up rivers and sought places for settlement. They came from a wooded, low-lying country, and so tended to settle in the well-timbered river valleys of this country. The mystery of the forests was associated with their religion. They were also afraid of meres or marshes which were the haunts of dragons and evil powers. They were suspicious of Roman towns and unattracted by the remains of civilisation. For a time these fell into decay, inhabited by squatters, but in time they returned to use as Christian and administrative centres dependent again on the roads. For the most part, the Saxons found their own places of settlement, villages named after the settlers. For the first time we have the personal name as opposed to that of a Roman community centre. The Saxons started clearing the forest and cultivating the heavy soil of river valleys with the heavy ox-drawn plough. A new pattern of settlement took place of timbered huts in scattered villages. The hills and the rivers retain their ancient names, but the settlements take the names of new people.

"A British strain in the personal name of the Anglo-Saxons, especially visible in Northumbria, is witness to a certain amount of intermarriage." (D. Whitlock)

Place Names

The study of place names is fascinating. One has to take a work like Ekwall's 'Oxford Dictionary of Place Names' or Mawer's 'Place Names of Northumberland'. These works trace derivations and consider old spellings. This is not a matter of guesswork or speculation. The element 'inga' in a place name is an indication of a tribal or folk settlement, and there is possibly one in Northumberland, namely Birling, on the coast near Warkworth. Much more common is the element 'ing' as a possessive in association with 'ham' meaning abode or settlement. There are quite a number of these – Eglingham, Edlingham, Whittingham, Bellingham, Ovingham, Chillingham, Ellingham, Eltringham. With the exception of Bell, which may mean 'a hill', the others are derived from personal names. Ellingham is the ham of Edla's people, Ellington is the tun of Ella's people, Chillingham is the ham of Ceofel's people and Bedlington the tun of Bedla's people. Edlingham and Eglingham were associated with Eadwulf and Ecgwulf respectively. The term 'tun' has been introduced, a common term to denote a settlement and of later date than 'ham'. It is difficult to give these any date, only the 'ings' are considered early and the others cover a long period. But it seems that a very large proportion of place names in Northumberland are of Anglo-Saxon or Old English origin. There is a noticeable absence of Scandinavian names, but a considerable number of Norman French.

Cameron, in his book on place-names, gives a map showing that in the Lowland Zone of England, there are comparatively few rivers with Celtic names. In the second area beyond the Jurassic Ridge but including Northumbria, there is a very strong survival of Celtic river names. The third zone, the far West, is almost completely Celtic. It has to be remembered that Celtic names were used for later settlements – a settlement might take a river's name, and it must not therefore be assumed that it is very ancient. There can be historical proof to the contrary.

There are, of course, combination names where elements of two languages are combined. Examples are Kirkley and Kirkheaton. The 'kirk' element is misleading since one assumes the association of 'church' which is correct in many examples. But there 'kirk' is derived from the British word 'cruc' meaning hill, so that Kirkley really means hill-hill in British and Old English. Similarly, Kirkheaton is 'the hill on high ground', another duplication. Capheaton is 'the chief tun situated on high ground'.

The river Aln (British name) has Alnham, Alnwick and Alnmouth, all settlements. The Alwin (British) has its tun and Cambois (British) is 'a bay' despite its French appearance. Callaly is Calfaleah, the pasture for calves, but Cowpen is the place of coops for catching fish and not a cattle enclosure. There are associations with 'bees'. Beal is 'beehill', Bickerton is the 'tun of the beekeepers' and Bewick is Bewic or Beefarm. Broom occurs at Broomhill, but also at Brandon and Branton. Ashington is Essenden, Old English meaning 'the vale overgrown with ash' – trees, not pit heaps. Barmoor is 'cranberry moor' and Barrasford is the 'ford by the grove'. Bolam is a place of trees, for bol means trunk. Blagdon is the 'black valley', and by contrast Birtley is the 'bright leah'. Bitchfield is 'beechfield' as at present pronounced, and Acomb is the plural of 'oak'. Benwell was 'within the wall' Roman, which ended at Wallsend. The term 'Botl' means a dwelling as in Shilbottle. The word 'burn' is often used for stream or spring and is Old English, but 'beck' found in the West is Scandinavian. Place names are the foundations of English history since they associate persons and places, also introducing a certain amount of topography and information on occupations. Farming was very much the basis of Anglo-Saxon society, when the wanderers had settled.

The Contest of Kings

In Northumberland one imagines the Anglo-Saxons securing places on the coast like Bamburgh, Lindisfarne, and the mouths of Coquet and Tyne, defensible against enemy attacks. The weakness of the Britons was that they could not remain united. After Ida's time, Welsh tradition was that the Kings of North Britain joined in a long and bitter struggle against the invaders, and a Saxon King was closely besieged on Lindisfarne. But there was also danger to the Britons from the Yorkshire settlements, and about 600 A.D. there was a great gathering of the Britons making a common cause against the invader. A battle was fought at Catraeth, probably Catterick, and on this hung the fate of the North. The combined forces of the Britons were defeated. This is not mentioned in the Anglo-Saxon Chronicle, which observes that in 560 Aelle became King of the Northumbrians, and that in 565 Columba came from Ireland to Britain to instruct the Picts, and built a monastery at Iona. There is also the evidence that "*the South Picts had been baptised a long time before. Bishop Ninian had preached to them. He was educated in Rome, and his church and monastery is at Whithorn...”*

About this time Angles were seen in the Roman slave market. It was not unusual for war captives to be sold into slavery, and Patrick *c.*450 in a letter to Coroticus, a King of the Britons, condemned raids on the Irish coast for enslaving Irish Christians.

Both the Anglo-Saxon Chronicle and Welsh tradition recall another disaster for the Britons. Aethelfrith (593–616) had become King of Bernicia, and his victories raised Northumbria to a position of supremacy in the country. He fought against both the Scots and the Welsh. In 603 there was a great battle at Degsastan (probably Dawston) in Liddesdale.

"In this year Aedan, King of the Scots, fought along with the people of Dal Riada (Argyll) against Aethelfrith, King of the Northumbrians, at Degsastan, and almost all of his army was slain. There Theobald, Aethelfrith's brother, was slain with all his troops. No king of the Scots dared afterwards lead an army against this nation. Hering, son of Hussa, led the army thither."

Aethelfrith was the son of Aethelric, who was the son of Ida. It seems that earlier battles had led to the defeat of the Kings of Strathclyde and Rheged, bringing Aedan and Aethelfrith into conflict. Aethelfrith won another great victory over the Britons at Chester. The Anglo-Saxon Chronicle gives the date 605. In this year Pope Gregory passed away. In the same year Aethelfrith led his levies to Chester and there slew a countless number of Welsh: and so Augustine's prophecy was fulfilled which he spoke:

"If the Welsh refuse peace with us, they shall perish at the hands of the Saxons. Two hundred priests were also slain there who had come thither to pray for the Welsh host. Their leader was called Brocmail, who was one of the fifty who escaped thence." (Gregory was the monk who saw the Angle slaves in Rome, and afterwards sent Augustine to England.)

Shortly before this event Aethelfrith had made himself King of all Northumbria by conquering the kingdom of Deira and the boy king Edwin, son of Aelle, was driven into exile at the court of Raedwald, King of East Anglia. Aethelfrith married Aelle's daughter to help secure his position. Raedwald saw the danger of Aethelfrith's power and not only refused to hand Edwin over, but prepared to help him recover his lost kingdom. It is important to remember that Edwin had this stay in E. Anglia. Raedwald's palace was at Rendlesham, and the Sutton Hoo ship burial was not far away.

In 617 Aethelbert, King of Kent, died.

"In this year Aethelfrith, King of the Northumbrians, was killed by Raedwald, King of the East Angles, and Edwin, the son of Aelle, succeeded to the kingdom and conquered all Britain except Kent alone and drove out the princes, the sons of Aethelfrith." They took refuge in the North, and this explains their Ionian

Christianity. King Edwin is renowned as the first Christian King of Northumbria, and in addition secured the supremacy of his kingdom.

At this stage various forms of evidence can be brought together – place names, histories and chronicles, but more particularly archaeology. The Anglo-Saxon period was singularly lacking in the North in this respect because of the absence of cemeteries and other tangible remains. To some extent this has been modified by air photography which has revealed a number of sites, and by excavation which has shown that there are very considerable remains to be discovered. Timber remains do in fact leave traces that can be interpreted. There is evidence of Saxon occupation at Bamburgh, Yeavering and Tynemouth.

Air Photography and Edwin's Palace

Air photography is one of the most important methods used in the last forty years for obtaining information for all kinds of purposes – military survey and map making, landscape, vegetation and human settlement. It has been particularly important for archaeology, especially in areas that have been much subject to the plough. With so much land being converted to non-farming purposes, these surveys are most important. A certain amount can be revealed to the casual observer on foot, and a good deal more to the expert – mounds, banks, hollows and pits indicating the past activities. The late sloping rays of the winter sun shining on a landscape from which the herbage has been grazed or on which the bracken has died, reveals a whole pattern or set of patterns of human activity. It is a palimpsest, pattern upon pattern, and the earth reveals its secrets.

The greedy plough had bitten far into the hillsides when upland fields provided corn in medieval times or when high prices could be obtained in the Napoleonic Wars for feeding hungry millions. The present day demand for barley brings the plough into unaccustomed fields, and the tractor does not entirely obliterate the old ridge and furrow. This pattern is revealed by the crop itself. Where the hollows were the soil is deep, and the corn grows longer and greener: where the humps were the soil is not so deep, and the corn grows slightly shorter, is less green and tends to ripen earlier. In a windy, wet season the long corn gets flattened and the pattern is made plain.

So much is visible from the earth, but the air photograph reveals a great deal more, whether in black and white or in colour. In a dry summer all kinds of sites are revealed. Where the structure was a substantial one of stone and has disappeared, the foundations of the walls remain, and the soil above is shallow, so that in a dry year the vegetation becomes prematurely brown. In trenches that have been naturally filled in process of time, the soil produces lush green vegetation. Where a timber building has been burnt, the pattern can be seen even more clearly for buildings of timber require post holes or trenches. Places like the Roman town of

16

Silchester, which has not been built over, reveal a complete plan to air photography. Another site mapped in this way was the legionary fort at Inchtuthil, which was entirely of timber.

For us in the North the most important was the discovery of a site at Yeavering. Two sites were photographed in Glendale as possible monastic sites by Dr St Joseph, and appeared in his book 'Monastic Sites from the Air.' The one at Yeavering lay in the valley beneath the shadow of Yeavering Bell, the earlier native oppidum. A quarry, which has since become disused, was threatening the site, and excavations were carried out by Mr B. Hope-Taylor. The site is marked on the Akeld Kirknewton road by a stone monument, since nothing appears of the old Gefrin in the field.

An excavation report appeared in 1977, and a great deal depends on plans and photographs. But it was a pioneer work in that the buildings were of timber, and yet a great deal was discovered. It could open a new phase in Anglo-Saxon archaeology since for hundreds of years, timber was the main material for halls, houses and churches, built by these peoples.

At Yeavering some of the rectangular crop marks of the air photographs were shown to be the palace of Edwin, King of Northumbria (616–633). This was an area of the greatest importance in the seventh century, the period of Northumbrian supremacy. Edwin's kingdom stretched from Edwin's burgh on the Forth to the Humber and included York. Yeavering was shown to be an important residence and place of assembly.

In excavation the removal of the turf revealed an area of sandy soil and stones. The drying-out process revealed the darker, deeper soil of the post holes and sleeper trenches of timber buildings.

It was found that the township existed before the time of Edwin. The first phase which had showed up on the photograph as a double crop mark was a fort of considerable size with double defences. The outer defence was a simple palisade, but the inner was double with a fighting platform. This was late sixth century in date and the township grew up outside in the early seventh century. Within this the first building had wall timbers of 20cm (8") thickness closely set together, and lined with wattle and daub which had been burnt hard.

There was no domestic refuse, but bones were found outside, and a grave to the south indicated that this was a pagan temple converted to later use as a Christian Church. Yet another rectangular building had been burnt and rebuilt. This had a later partition and there were indications of a box bed with postholes. Then there was a central complex of buildings, showing a good deal of rebuilding and extension. Photographs were taken of the various stages of excavation, and a great deal depended on the use of the relative humidity of the soils, with differing rates of drying, to obtain visible evidence.

17

An original rectangular building, measuring some 30m by 9 m (100 ft by 30 ft), had extensions at either end. Then a still larger building was constructed to the east but impinging on the first building. There were three stages of occupation, showing burning and rebuilding. Further enclosures, it was suggested, could be for tents or houses. Foundation trenches for the halls were at least 1m (3 ft) deep and the larger were as deep as 2m (7ft). The upright timbers were slotted – alternate ones did not go underground. Evidence was provided by burnt timber as well as the silted holes and trenches.

The growth of these timber buildings showed greater security in the reign of Aethelfrith, and the hall was increased in size. Serious destruction took place probably at the death of Edwin (632). Under Oswald the royal palace was rebuilt, only to be burnt again in 642 when Oswald was killed. The palace was again restored, but it seems to have been of lesser importance and was abandoned after 670, probably when Ecgfrith was killed in 685.

There was found a further structure of considerable interest from a complex of post holes. It was segmental in shape and consisted of nine concentric arcs, providing seating for a 'moot' or assembly. The focal point was a rostrum or platform. It was discovered that a series of six tiers of seating had been extended to nine at a later time. On either side there were wattle screens. This structure explains the importance of the place.

Yeavering was a place of meeting as well as a royal palace. Here important persons of the kingdom would meet the king in council. It was more important than either a banqueting hall or hunting lodge. Much is left to the imagination, since there is no superstructure, and 'Beowulf', a poem written in the north in the eighth century gives a picture of Heorot, the great Hall of Horthgar, which may apply to this.

"It came into his mind to command the erection of a building that should be the greatest banqueting hall ever known, in which he could apportion to young and old everything that God had entrusted to him, with the exception of public lands and human life... Tall and wide gabled, the hall towered overhead: yet it was to endure terrible and leaping flames... That resplendent building though secured inside with iron clamps, had been badly wrecked."

Those who could fashion timber ships such as that found at Sutton Hoo, were capable of making timber buildings of excellent workmanship. There was another Saxon palace excavated at Cheddar. Bede indicates that the Northumbrian kings had several such palaces – one on the Derwent near York, another near Doncaster and 'the royal country seat at Odgefrin' (Yeavering). Here the archaeological evidence fits in with the history of Northumbria as detailed by Bede. There were other sites at Mitfield and Dunbar.

18

Edwin, Oswald, Oswiu, Kings of Northumbria

It is perhaps rather strange to think of Northumbria having Foreign Policy, but in Edwin's reign this was of the greatest importance. He had to secure his kingdom against attack, and was involved in prolonged and distant campaigns. He was able to exercise supremacy over Mercia, and his power was sufficient to provoke other kings to contrive his death. The Anglo Saxon Chronicle records:

"In this year (626) Eomaer came from Cwichelm, King of the West Saxons, intending to stab to death King Edwin, but he stabbed his thegns Lilla and Forthhere and wounded the King. And the same night was born Edwin's daughter, who was called Eanflaed. Then the King promised that he would give his daughter to God, if he would by his prayers obtain from God that he might destroy his enemy who had sent the assassin thither. And he went into Wessex with an Army, and destroyed there five kings and killed many of that people."

This shows how a King had to face treachery and depended on the loyalty of his thegns. Considerations of religion had a practical basis and Edwin conquered under the sign of the Cross. He extended his authority by conquering Elmet, a British area east of the Pennines. He was able to penetrate the Aire Gap and defeat Cadwallon, King of Gwynedd in N. Wales. He overran Anglesey and took possession of the Isle of Man. Nor was he troubled by his northern neighbours, and Bede, looking back, regarded this as an era of good government. The concluding words of Beowulf might apply to Edwin *"of all kings he was the gentlest and most gracious of men, the kindest to his people and the most desirous of renown."*

Bede records too that like other leaders, Edwin had a standard always carried before him.

Edwin *"brought under his sway all the territories inhabited by the Britons"*. This shows the extent of his overlordship.

"In those parts of Britain under King Edwin's jurisdiction, the proverb still runs that a woman could carry her new-born babe across the island from sea to sea without any fear of harm. And such was the king's concern for the welfare of his people that in a number of places where he had noticed clear springs adjacent to the highway, he ordered posts to be erected with brass bowls hanging from them, so that travellers could drink and refresh themselves. And so great was the people's affection for him, and so great the awe in which he was held, that no one presumed to use these bowls for any other purpose. The king's dignity was highly respected throughout his realm, and whether in battle or in peaceful progress through city, town and countryside in the company of his thanes, the royal standard was always borne before him. And whenever he passed through the streets on foot, the standard known to the Romans as a Tufa, and to the English as a Tuf, was carried in front of him."

In his reign the country came nearer to unification than at any time since the Romans left, but more than this Edwin introduced Christianity to Northumbria. He had been influenced during his exile and more so by his marriage. Allied to Kent, he wished to marry Ethelbert's daughter, known as Ethburge or Tata, but Eadbald, her brother, was doubtful about a heathen marriage. Edwin offered her complete freedom to exercise her religion and expressed himself willing to accept Christianity. She went north accompanied by Paulinus, already a bishop, as her chaplain. Paulinus was described as "*a tall man having a slight stoop, with black hair, an ascetic face and a venerable and majestic presence.*"

With his providential escape from assassination, the successful birth of a daughter and with victory over his enemies, Edwin was more easily persuaded by Paulinus, who also knew of Edwin's exile. The King received a letter from Pope Boniface, and the Queen was urged "*to persevere in using every effort to soften his heart by teaching him the laws of God.*"

Edwin did not decide on his own account but summoned a Council of his wise men to discuss the matter. Coifi, the chief priest, took the lead in denouncing the old gods whom they had served without profit. One nobleman likened the life of man to the passing of a sparrow through the lighted banqueting hall on a winter evening.

"*Your Majesty, when we compare the present life of man with that time of which we have no knowledge, it seems to me like the swift flight of a lone sparrow through the banqueting-hall where you sit in the winter months to dine with your thanes and counsellors. Inside there is a comforting fire to warm the room; outside, the wintry storms of snow and rain are raging. This sparrow flies swiftly in through one door of the hall, and out through another. While he is inside, he is safe from the winter storms; but after a few moments of comfort, he vanishes from sight into the darkness whence he came. Similarly, man appears on earth for a little while, but we know nothing of what went before this life, and what follows. Therefore if this new teaching can reveal any more certain knowledge, it seems only right that we should follow it.*"

Paulinus spoke about the new religion, which was accepted.

Coifi dramatically started the destruction of the pagan temples. Brandishing a spear and riding a stallion (a priest should ride a mare and not bear arms), he attacked the idols.

"*When the crowd saw him they thought he had gone mad, but without hesitation, as soon as he reached the temple, he cast a spear into it and profaned it.*" Bede continues, "*So King Edwin with also his nobility and a large number of humbler folk, accepted the faith, and were washed in the cleansing waters of Baptism in the eleventh year of his reign, which was the year 627, and about one hundred and eighty years after the first arrival of the English in Britain. The King's baptism took place at York on Easter Day, the 12th of April, in the Church of St*

Peter the Apostle, which the King had built of timber during the time of his instruction and preparation for Baptism, and in this city he established the see of his teacher and Bishop Paulinus. Soon after his baptism, at Paulinus's suggestion, he gave orders to build on the same site a larger and more noble stone basilica, which was to enclose his earlier little oratory. The foundations were laid and the walls of a square church began to arise around the little oratory."

This was the process of the development of Christianity, first a building of timber and then of stone, and always a cross.

Meanwhile Paulinus with great missionary spirit travelled the kingdom. The association of baptism of many people at Holystone, Northumberland, is a mistaken reading, but Paulinus was at Yeavering. He *"accompanied the king and queen to the royal palace at Adgefrin, and remained there 36 days constantly occupied in instructing and baptising. During this period he did nothing from dawn to dusk but to proclaim Christ's saving message to the people, who gathered from all the surrounding villages and countryside: and when he had instructed them, he washed them in the cleansing waters of Baptism in the nearby River Glen. This country seat was abandoned by later kings, who built another at a place called Melmin."* (Millfield).

The nearest church to Yeavering, Kirknewton, hiding under the hills is an eloquent reminder of the coming of Christianity here. It has a thick walled ancient chancel and an even more ancient sculptured stone, showing the Adoration of the Magi.

Edwin's reign was soon to end; the Welsh King Cadwallon combined with Penda, the pagan King of Mercia, and invaded Northumbria. The battle took place somewhere in Hatfield Chase in 632. Edwin was killed and his army suffered severe defeat. Terrible devastation and slaughter took place in Northumbria. Bede condemns Cadwallon all the more strongly because he was supposed to be a Christian, yet destroyed Christian churches and people. Edwin's head was taken to York, where it was eventually placed in the Church. Two of his sons were killed, but his wife and Bishop Paulinus with the rest of the family, managed to escape taking much plate with them. Bede mentions *"a great cross of gold and a golden chalice hallowed for the use of the altar"*, which were taken to Kent.

Northumbria was again divided. Osric, son of Elfric, ruled Deira: Eanfrid, son of Ethelfrid, became King of Bernicia. But they too were defeated by Cadwallon. Bede regards this as retribution for their reversion to idolatry, and Cadwallon continued his tyranny of the North. But late in the year 633 he was overcome in battle at Heavenfield, near Hexham. The site is now marked by a wooden cross almost on the line of the Roman Wall. Oswald, the victor, was a Christian prince of Bernicia, who had lived at Iona while in exile. Though his men were fewer in number, they prayed together before battle and attacked at dawn. A church was built on the site and it became a place of pilgrimage, dedicated to St Oswald.

The defeat of Edwin had separated Northumbria from relations with the Roman Church as established in Kent, and in the years that followed there was to be a change in the direction of enlightenment. For Oswald had been in Iona, and it was to Iona he turned for help in bringing back Christianity to Northumbria.

The man who eventually came was Bishop Aidan, and he was given the island of Lindisfarne as his see. Since he was not yet proficient in the English language, King Oswald often enjoyed the task of interpreting the word of God to his thegns.

Oswald restored the authority of Northumbria. He was on friendly terms with Kent and he himself married a daughter of the house of Wessex. Oswald also exercised dominion over the South Picts and the Scots. Irish annals record a siege of Edinburgh in 638, when he recovered and extended his frontier to the Firth of Forth. His period of power was brought to a premature end by his death in battle against Penda of Mercia at Maserfelth (probably Oswestry) in 641, *"on the 5th of April and his body was buried at Bardney. His holiness and miracles were afterwards abundantly made manifest throughout this island and his hands are at Bamburgh uncorrupted."* Bede explains that a generous act of the king was blessed by Aidan, who took his right hand and said, *"May this hand never perish."*

"Later events prove that his prayer was heard, for when Oswald was killed in battle, his right hand and arm were severed from his body, and remain uncorrupted to this day. They are preserved as venerated relics in a silver casket at the church of St Peter in the royal city, which is called Bebba (Bamburgh) after a former queen. It is said that Oswald often remained in prayer from the early hour of Lauds until dawn, and that through his practice of constant prayer and thanksgiving to God, he always sat with his hands palm upwards on his knees. It is also said, and has since become a proverb, that 'his life closed in prayer'; for when he saw the enemy forces surrounding him and knew that his end was near, he prayed for the souls of his soldiers, saying as he fell, 'God have mercy on their souls'. As I have already mentioned, his bones were taken up and buried in the Abbey of Bardney; but the king who slew him ordered that his head, hands and arms be hacked off and fixed on stakes. The following year, Oswald's successor Oswy came to the place with his army, and removed them, placing the head in the church at Lindisfarne, and the hands and arms in his own royal city of Bamburgh."

Bede remarks of Aidan – *"His life was in marked contrast to the apathy of our times."* He was kind and generous, and simple in his teaching. A predecessor found that the Northern English refused to listen to him. *"He returned home and reported to his superiors that he had been unable to teach anything to the nation to whom they had sent him because they were an uncivilized people of an obstinate and barbarous temperament."* But Aidan convinced them by his outspokenness against wrongdoers even though they were wealthy, and by his own example. If he obtained gifts of money, he used them to redeem slaves from captivity.

The death of Oswald was a severe blow to Northumbria and to Christianity. Bede gives some idea of the situation: *"The Mercians spread ruin far and wide throughout Northumbria and reached the very gates of the royal city.* (Bamburgh) *Unable to enter it by force or after a siege, Penda attempted to set fire to it."* He pulled down the neighbouring villages, and stacked the timber against the city wall on the landward side. But Aidan who was on Farne Island prayed to God for help, and the wind changed, blowing the fire against the attackers.

After Oswald's death, Deira was ruled by Oswine, one of Edwin's royal line. He was very religious, and ruled for nine years. He was then treacherously killed by Oswiu, who ruled over the more northerly kingdom. It had to be remembered that there was often joint kingship in an area, and members of a royal family could be regarded as kings. Sometimes one king eliminated the others as here, Oswiu got rid of Oswine. Aidan died in the same year (651).

"Death came to Aidan in the 16th year of our episcopate when he was staying at the king's country house near the capital. Having a church and a lodging there, Aidan often used to go and stay at the place, travelling about the surrounding countryside to preach. This was his practice at all the King's country seats, for he had no personal possessions except his church and a few fields around it. When he fell ill a tent was erected for him against the west wall of the church and it so happened that as he drew his last breath he was leaning against a post that strengthened the outer wall. He passed away on the last day of August... and his body was soon taken across to Lindisfarne Island and buried in the Monks' cemetery. When a larger church, dedicated to the most blessed Prince of the Apostles, was built there some while later, his bones were transferred to it and buried at the right side of the altar in accordance with the honours due to so great a prelate."

This extract is of some interest as showing that the king, as did later medieval kings, moved from place to place to make use of produce. Land was granted by the king to thegns and also to the Church. The Bishop too moved about, and often stayed at these royal country houses. Of interest, too, is the fact that the church mentioned was of timber. *"Some years later Penda, King of Mercia, came and destroyed everything that he found with fire and sword, and he burned down the village and the Church where Aidan had died."* But the beam on which Aidan had leaned was preserved in this and yet a later fire. (If the beam were a timber support and external – the building could be burnt and this left standing.)

The death of Oswine did not enable Oswiu to take over Deira. Another king was chosen who had the support of Penda of Mercia. A son of Penda, Peada by name, whom his father appointed to a throne – that of the Middle Angles, wanted to marry Elfleda, Oswiu's daughter. In order to do this he was prepared to become a

23

Christian. He was influenced by Alfrid, Oswiu's son, who was married to Cyneburga, Penda's daughter.

"Accordingly, Peada was baptised by Bishop Finan, together with his companions, thanes and servants, at a well-known village belonging to the King known as At-wall." (This is Wall, near Hexham, where the King had a palace.) Four priests chosen for their learning and piety went with him and one was Adda, brother of Utta, Abbot of Gateshead.

Penda continued to be extremely powerful, campaigning against Wessex and killing King Anna of E. Anglia. He also raided Northumbria, and in 654 contrived a coalition, which included the new King of the East Angles and several British princes, to crush Oswiu. He had a vast army, 'thirty legions' strong, and Oswiu with a much smaller force was compelled to retreat. However, putting his trust in God, he fought back and was able to defeat Penda at Winwaed, which is thought to be in the neighbourhood of Leeds. Penda and Ethelhere were killed and many men were lost, especially because the river was in flood. Oswiu had promised his daughter to God, and she, Elfleda, entered the monastery at Hartlepool under Abbess Hilda. Another monastery was founded at Whitby, and here Elfleda became a novice. Here she was to live for some 50 years and became *"a mistress of the monastic life."*

Oswiu also helped Peada, whom he allowed to rule Southern Mercia, to establish a monastery at Peterborough. Oswiu was the third and last of the Northumbrian Bretwaldas or rulers of Britain. Peada did not live long. *"In the following spring (65) however, during the Festival of Easter, Peada was foully assassinated through the treachery, it is said, of his wife."* The Anglo-Saxon Chronicle puts it laconically: *"But that King Peada did not reign for long, for he was betrayed by his own queen at Eastertide."* Wulfhere, son of Penda, succeeded him, and completed the abbey at Peterborough. One of the witnesses who signed with his cross was *"Oswiu, king of Northumbria and friend of this monastery"*. The monastery was an essential element in the spread and maintenance of Christianity.

Bede indicates that Mercians had recovered their freedom under Wulfhere and accepted Christianity on their own account. Wulfhere perhaps nominally accepted Oswiu and was much engaged in fighting against the Britons and the Isle of Wight. In 664 the Anglo-Saxon Chronicle mentions an eclipse of the sun and a great pestilence. Almost casually: *"Colman with his companions went to his native land."* This was one of the most important events in the history of the Church in Northumbria, and Bede depicts it in some detail. The other side of the picture to Colman's departure was the triumph of Rome in the person of Wilfrid. The great influence from this time was to be from the South and not from the North.

24

PROBLEMS OF RELIGION

At this date, 663, the greater part of the country had been converted to Christianity. No doubt there were still pagan backwaters and abodes of superstition with simple people somewhat adrift. Conversion to Christianity, generally through the agency of the royal court, was followed by the erection of churches and monasteries, which became centres of learning. English laws became written for the first time, and the warrior or hero of a story tends to acquire saintly virtues. In place of pagan shrines arose wonderfully carved free-standing Christian crosses, three times a man's height, and advertising the new religion. People at first, no doubt, were reluctant to submit to the confines of a building where magic might be practised on them.

The spread of Christianity brought the Roman and Celtic Churches into direct conflict. Christianity had continued in the West after the Saxon invasions, but it was increasingly difficult to keep contact with Rome. The Celtic Church had developed its own customs such as were convenient to remote countries with inclement climate. An Irish monastery with its beehive huts would appear very primitive to a Roman. But there could be no doubt of the piety of such men as Patrick, Columba and Aidan. With the coming of Augustine to Kent in 597, Canterbury became the Christian centre in the South of England, always in direct contact with Rome. Augustine himself experienced difficulties.

Christianity was introduced to Northumbria from Kent, but after the death of Edwin conversion came from Iona. Contacts with Kent were maintained and Eanfled, wife to King Oswiu, was brought up in Kent, though a daughter of Edwin. Christian differences divided Northumbria and the royal household. There were several of these – firstly the tonsure, the sign of the religious. We are told of Wilfrid: *"He had an ardent desire to receive St Peter's, that is, the Roman form of tonsure which goes right round the head in the shape of Christ's own crown of thorns."* This he obtained on a visit to Rome. The Celtic method was to shave the top of the head, leaving a fringe at the front and a lot of hair at the back.

A second difference was the organisation and very building of the church itself. Christians like Wilfrid and Benedict Biscop, who had been to Rome, could not be content with small wooden churches. Bede says of Finan, who succeeded Aidan at Lindisfarne, *"He built a church in the Isle of Lindisfarne, his see, constructing it not of stone, but of hewn oak thatched with reeds after the Scots manner. It was later dedicated by the most reverend Archbishop Theodore in honour of the blessed Apostle St Peter. But Eadbert, a later Bishop of Lindisfarne, removed the thatch and covered both roof and walls with sheets of lead."* Also the Celtic priests and monks did a great deal of wandering, desirable in times of missionary zeal, but settled communities would need more permanent arrangements.

The final cause of division was the date of Easter – this was the one thing Bede had against Aidan. Aidan was patient, but Colman the Scot who succeeded Finan was an uncompromising supporter of the Celtic customs. King Oswiu preferred the Scots' teaching, but his wife and his son Alfrid *"rightly regarded Wilfrid's teaching as superior to all the tradition of the Scots."* There was confusion at Court, and Easter was celebrated twice according to both customs. For Christmas this would have been no matter – two occasions for rejoicing, but for Easter it was disconcerting. *"When the King had ended Lent and was keeping Easter, the Queen and her attendants were still fasting and keeping Palm Sunday."* These matters and differences of ritual must have provoked immense hostility.

The King decided to call a Conference or Synod at Whitby (in 663), where the Abbess Hilda had a monastery for both women and men. Ruins of this underlie the present monastic remains. Those present were King Oswiu and his son, also the King of Wessex and his son, with Bishop Agilberht of Paris. Cedd, formerly of Northumbria, but now Bishop of the East Saxons, acted as interpreter. The main protagonists were Colman the Scot, who put forward the traditions of the Church, of Columba and of St John, the beloved Apostle, against Wilfrid who argued for Rome. These practices he said were universal. *"The only people who were stupid enough to disagree are these Scots and their obstinate adherents the Picts and the Britons, who inhabit only a proportion of these two islands in the remote ocean."* Against St John he quoted the authority of St Peter. *"Thou art Peter and upon this rock I will build my church and the gates of hell shall not prevail against it, and to thee I will give the keys of the kingdom of heaven."*

Both sides accepted the authority of this saying. *"At this the King concluded 'Then I tell you Peter is the guardian of the gates of Heaven and I shall not contradict him. I shall obey his commands in everything to the best of my knowledge and ability, otherwise when I come to the gates of heaven, he who holds the keys may not be willing to open them.'"* When Colman and the Scots left, Tuda became Bishop of the Northumbrians and Eata from Melrose became Abbot of Lindisfarne.

"So frugal and austere were Colman and his predecessors that when they left the monastery there were very few buildings except the church; indeed, no more than met their bare requirements. They had no property except cattle, and whenever they received any money from rich folk, they immediately gave it to the poor; for they had no need to acquire money or provide lodgings for important people, since such only visited the church in order to pray or hear the word of God. Whenever opportunity offered, the king himself used to come with only five or six attendants, and when he had visited the church to pray, he used to leave. But if they happened to remain for a meal, they were content with the plain daily food of the brothers and asked nothing more, for the sole concern of these teachers was to serve God, not the world; to satisfy the soul not the belly. Accordingly the religious habit was held in

high esteem, and whenever any priest or monk paid a visit, he was joyfully welcomed by all as the servant of God. And if anyone met him on the road, they ran to him and bowed, eager to be signed by his hand or receive a blessing from his lips. Whenever he spoke, he was given an attentive hearing, and on Sundays the people flocked to the churches and monasteries, not to obtain food, but to hear the word of God taught. When a priest visited a village, the people were quick to gather in some cottage to hear the word of life, for priests and clerics always came to a village solely to preach, baptize, visit the sick, and, in short, to care for the souls of its people. They were so free from the sin of avarice that none of them would accept lands or gifts for the buildings of monasteries unless expressly directed to do so by the secular authorities. This was the general practice for many years among the churches of Northumbria. But enough has been said on such matters." Bede.*

But the Synod of Whitby did not produce immediate order. Difficulties were the rivalries of kings and the pretensions of bishops. On the death of Tuda, King Alfrid of Deira sent Wilfrid to Agilberht, who was now Bishop of Paris, to be consecrated as Bishop. Wilfrid remained overseas for some time, and Oswiu sent Chad, brother of Cedd and Abbot of Lastingham, to Canterbury to be consecrated Bishop of York. This was done by Bishop Wini of the West Saxons.

Chad *"travelled on foot and not on horseback when he went to preach the Gospel, whether in towns or in the countryside cottages, villages or castles, for he was one of Aidan's disciples... And when Wilfrid returned to Britain as a Bishop, he introduced into the English churches many Catholic customs..."* In fact Wilfrid's return was marked by conflict and his biographer, Eddius Stephanus, goes to great trouble to defend him. Wilfrid regarded his province as equivalent to the later Archbishopric of York, and these pretensions were not acceptable.

This was a period of pestilence, and among those who died was Archbishop Deusdedit and King Eorcenberht of Kent. His successor, Egbert and King Oswiu conferred together, and decided to send Widheard to Rome to be consecrated Archbishop so that *"he could consecrate Catholic Bishops for the churches of the English throughout Britain"*. Widheard died before he could return, and the Pope made a wise choice in appointing Theodore of Tarsus to be Archbishop. He came in 669, together with Hadrian, and their escort was none other than Benedict Biscop, a Northumbrian nobleman who was again in Rome. He was a strong supporter of Rome, and the founder of the monasteries of Monkwearmouth and Jarrow.

Theodore held the see of Canterbury for twenty years, and his work was to be the proper organisation of the Church of England, which he did by constant labour and by holding regular meetings with the clergy. His diocesan system was to bring stability, and within this framework non-monastic churches were encouraged and established. The task was more difficult because plague had carried off many clergy and some areas reverted to paganism. Theodore visited each part of the country in turn, and was determined to reduce the size of the sees. East Anglia was divided into Dunwich and Elmham, Mercia had Lichfield, Worcester and Hereford, Northumbria had York, Lindisfarne, Hexham and Abercorn. The last area was lost to the Picts and Lindsey to Mercia by Northumbria.

There was as yet no parochial system established. The incomes of churches were from dues and endowments. Churches and monasteries were regarded as the property of their founders. Bede indicated that they might be founded to evade royal dues or to provide positions for members of a family. On the other hand, the rapid growth of monastic life was instrumental in achieving a high level of education and learning.

The contributions of some of the great Northumbrians might be briefly mentioned. Two of these were born in 634 – Cuthbert and Wilfrid. Although Cuthbert is claimed by Durham, he spent a great deal of his life in Northumberland and died on the Inner Farne. Wilfrid covers a much wider field. To a large extent Cuthbert represents the spirit and traditions of the Celtic Church, Wilfrid the organisation and church building of Rome. Bede produced a 'Life of St Cuthbert', based on an anonymous life, which was not well written.

Cuthbert and Wilfrid

Cuthbert's early life was spent on the Scottish border and he was a healthy active boy, taking a leading part in all sports and games, until he was once reproved by a very small child for wasting his time. Later through some kind of prophetic vision he saw Aidan's death at Bamburgh, and went into the monastery at Melrose. Boisil, the Prior, as Cuthbert approached on horseback, exclaimed, *"Behold the servant of the Lord."*

"Once admitted, Cuthbert was careful to keep up with the rest in observing the rule. He excelled them all in his zeal for discipline. He watched, prayed, worked and read harder than anyone else."

After some years at Ripon, he returned to Melrose, which was afflicted by the plague. Cuthbert recovered, but Boisil was seriously ill and spent his last days instructing Cuthbert. Cuthbert became Prior of Melrose on Boisil's death. In the monastery he set a fine example to his monks, but he also went out on foot or on horse teaching and preaching. *"He was so keen to preach that sometimes he would be away for a whole week or a fortnight or even a month, living with the rough hill folk, preaching and calling them heavenward by his example."*

He visited Coldingham where the abbess was Ebba, Oswiu's sister, and found affairs well conducted. Next he became Prior of Lindisfarne, and here found that Benedict's rule was not so strictly kept. But he persisted despite the arguments of the monks, and won them over by patience and example. He visited the mainland including the royal palace of Bamburgh. At Lindisfarne: *"The Episcopal residence and the monastery are one and the same, and all the clergy and the monks."*

Cuthbert next adopted the life of a hermit on the Farne Islands, which were believed to be a haunt of devils. He built a hut with stone walls 7.5m (25 ft) diameter and higher than a man. The roof was of timber and straw. There was a larger hut for visitors and a place for prayer. He is said not to have removed his boots from Easter to Easter, and then only for ceremonial washing. He dug a well and grew barley. His presence attracted many people and miracles were attributed to him. He cured Elfled, daughter of Oswiu and Abbess of Whitby, whom he met at Coquet Island. This shows Cuthbert was not opposed to women and incidentally illustrates the importance of travel by sea in those times.

He was next appointed Bishop of Lindisfarne, *"Letters and messengers were sent to him repeatedly, but he refused to move."* 'King Ecgfrith and Bishop Trumwine had to cross over and plead with him before he consented.

"They kneel, they weep, they entreat him to leave his oratory. Cuthbert also weeps. At last he yields and the holy man some months later is conducted to the great church at York, and is there consecrated with pomp by Archbishop Theodore. This ceremony performed on Easter Day 685 is memorable. It is the climax that precedes the decline of Northumbrian greatness: it is a visible meeting-point of the old and the new, of Scottish and Mediterranean religion.

The cathedral in which the anchorite was consecrated had been begun by Paulinus. It had been completed by Wilfrid, who had whitewashed its walls, refurbished its altars, covered the ridges of the roof with lead and glazed the windows to keep out the birds. (That was Wilfrid's way. Cuthbert on his island had made it his custom to talk to the birds; on one occasion to condemn them; in nomine Jesu Christi.)

The two men before the altar are a notable conjunction of the East and the West. Theodore, the native of Tarsus, once student at Athens, now emissary of Rome, statesman, successful administrator, maker of laws, placing his hand on the head of Cuthbert, once shepherd of Tweedale, haggard and unkempt as on his lonely rock, an ascetic who starved himself on a diet of barley and onions and who, for all his Catholic orthodoxy on the Easter question, still has the soul of a Celtic anchorite. And round these two and five other assistant bishops stand King Ecgfrith, his high reeve and band of thanes. The minds of these are filled with the thoughts of military glory and the conquests to be won in the North." (Hodgkin)

Wilfrid was away appealing to Rome. Bishop Eata had to be transferred from Lindisfarne to make way for Cuthbert. Wilfrid's supporters regarded the infirmity of Elfled and the calamity of Ecgfrith as just punishment for opposing him. Cuthbert held his great office with holiness and humility. He visited various parts of his diocese and while looking at the Roman ruins at Carlisle in the presence of the

Queen, he had another forewarning of death. *"Oh. Oh. Oh I think the battle is finished."* A few days later came the news Ecgfrith had fallen while fighting the Picts and his army had suffered severely. He had been king for 15 years, and was succeeded by his brother Aldfrith.

Cuthbert returned to the Inner Farne after a time and fell ill. He refused to be attended upon and Abbot Herefrith found him near to death. He died, and on March 20th 687 he was taken to Lindisfarne for burial. He was buried in a stone coffin, and eleven years later when his corpse was transferred to a wooden coffin it was found to be intact. Cuthbert was to become famous as a miracle working saint. His bones were moved in face of Danish threats, and travelled about the north country, finally finding a resting-place at Durham. Cuthbert represents the same strain in Christianity as St Francis of Assisi.

Wilfrid was very different, and so was his achievement. He was the son of a considerable landowner, and presented himself as a youth before Queen Eanfled, Oswiu's queen. With her advice and protection he took the service of God, serving a nobleman, Cudda, who decided to take up monastic life at Lindisfarne. Wilfrid wished to visit Rome, and was again helped by the Queen to achieve his desire. He received the tonsure in Rome, returning to England with relics in his hands, and in his mind impressions made by Roman churches. He was welcomed by Aldfrith, who ruled Deira along with Oswiu his father, and was given the monastery of Ripon. He was also ordained a priest. His next achievement was at the Synod of Whitby in 663, where he won the victory for Rome. Colman departed from his see and Wilfrid was elected to take his place. He chose to seek consecration abroad, favouring a more direct link with Rome. *"He was attended by a retinue of 120 armed followers. He was borne aloft on a golden throne by nine bishops, to the accompaniment of songs and canticles from the choir."*

On his return Wilfrid claimed to rule the Bishopric of York, which *"consisted of all the lands of the Northumbrians and Picts to the borders of Oswiu's realms."* But in his absence Oswiu had installed Chad. *"This Chad, a Celt but a truly devout servant of God and a great teacher, was ordained in complete defiance of canon law. Wilfrid knew nothing of the whole affair."* But he showed moderation and was content to return to Ripon. He also had connections with Mercia. He was re-installed in 669 by Theodore of Tarsus, and in 675 *"I, Wilfrid, archbishop of York, am a witness to this charter..."* denotes his dignity. His territory extended over Deira, Bernicia and Lindsey. This was his period of greatness. He restored the Church at York, which he found in a decayed state. It is interesting to note that to this time the windows had no glass and so the birds could not be excluded. He also built and dedicated a Church at Ripon. Ecgfrith's conquests at the expense of the Picts and Mercia enlarged Wilfrid's sphere of influence. He encouraged the building of churches, and also the spread of sacred music.

Eddius Stephanus, who wrote the 'Life of Wilfrid', was a singing master. Eddius writes of Hexham Church which was built in 672–8 : *"At Hexham he built a church to the glory of God and honour of St Andrew on land given by the saintly Queen Aethulthryth. My poor mind is quite at a loss for words to describe it – the great depth of the foundations, the crypts of beautifully dressed stone, the vast structure supported by columns of various styles with numerous side aisles, the walls of remarkable height and length, the many winding passages and spiral staircases leading up and down. Without a doubt it was the Spirit of God who taught the Bishop to plan the construction of such a place, for we have never heard of its like this side of the Alps. Bishop Acca, who by God's grace is still with us, decked out this superb edifice with splendid gold and silver ornaments, precious stones and silks and purple for the altars. What description could do justice to the fabric he installed."*

Hexham Church was undoubtedly the finest piece of building since the time of the Romans. Above ground it has disappeared, but beneath the present floor can be found Wilfrid's crypt, where precious relics were kept. The building stone was from the neighbouring Roman Wall and fort. A partly erased inscription is a reminder of Roman imperial quarrels, and the builder of Hexham himself was much engaged in controversy.

King Ecgfrid had married Ethelreda (St Audrey), daughter of Anna, King of the East Angles. She was extremely religious and eventually persuaded the King to allow her to retire to Coldingham, where Ecgfrid's aunt Ebba was Abbess. *"She received the veil and clothing of a nun from the hands of Bishop Wilfrid."* She was to become Abbess of Ely. Coldingham was later destroyed by fire, and a priest Edgils reported to Bede that it was God's punishment for their sins. *"Even the cells, which were built for prayer and study, are now converted into places for eating, drinking, gossip and other amusements. When they have leisure, even the nuns vowed to God abandon the propriety of their calling, and spend their time weaving fine clothes, which they employ to the peril of their souls, either to adorn themselves like brides or to attract the attention of strange men."*

Ecgfrith's new Queen Iurminburgh was said by Eddius to be jealous of Wilfrid *"She used all her eloquence to describe to Ecgfrith all St Wilfrid's temporal glories, listing his possessions, the number of his monasteries, the vastness of the buildings, his countless followers arrayed and armed like a king's retinue."* A baseless charge is made that Theodore was won over by bribes. In fact he probably saw that Wilfrid's territory was far too large and that some reorganisation was necessary. There was the problem of the local relationship of ruler and bishop, the position of the archbishop and the authority of Rome. Bede recalls that in 678 Wilfrid was driven out and two bishops replaced him – Bora Bishop of Deira at York, and Eata Bishop of Bernicia at Hexham or Lindisfarne. Eadhed was made Bishop of Lindsey, territory conquered by Ecgfrith from Mercia. Theodore consecrated these three at York and later two others – Tunbert to Hexham and Trumwin to be Bishop of the Picts, who were then subject to the English rule. Theodore probably realised that an empirical approach was necessary, and dioceses could not be finally fixed.

Wilfrid, to his credit, spent his time in missionary activities in Frisia and among the South Saxons. The winter of 679–80 was spent at Rome, where he obtained a papal decree for his restoration. He also brought back many relics and ornaments for his churches. But the Northumbrian King and his counsellors had no intention of submitting to papal decree, and *"Wilfrid was condemned to prison for nine months, there to be kept without any mark of honour to his rank."*

It is a good example of the conflict of authority between Pope and King, that was to persist till the time of Henry VIII. It is rather strange to think of Wilfrid in a prison cell, a change for the traveller, while Cuthbert emerged from his retreat for a brief moment of worldly glory. To pass the time of captivity, Wilfrid sang psalms, but he refused to compromise on the size of his diocese. According to Eddius he was released because of illness of the queen and he went into exile, continuing his missionary activities. In 685 he was reconciled to King Aldfrith, the successor of Ecgfrith. He was allowed to keep Hexham, Ripon and York, but it seems he was not fully reconciled. In 692 he again went into exile, and found a home in Mercia, where he did missionary work.

Ten years later the Synod of Austerfield (Bawtry) upheld the decrees of Archbishop Theodore, and Wilfrid, though an old man, again made the journey to Rome, and returned with fresh papal decrees. In 705 the death of Aldfrith made a compromise possible. Wilfrid was restored to Hexham and Ripon, where he spent his last years in comparative peace, dying in 709 at Oundle. Characteristic of him during his last days was the counting out of his wealth, dividing and setting it to different purposes. He was buried at Ripon.

His position in history is assured by Ennius's eulogistic biography. On the other hand, his achievement was important. Like Becket he stood against the King, though as much for personal reasons as for the Church. He helped to bring order into the Church and music into the services; he also employed men skilled in architecture and sculpture. He was personally fearless and showed great missionary fervour. There was something of the Christian Warrior about him, and he realised that treasures were necessary for the continuation of the work of the Church Monasteries and learning depended upon this wealth.

Benedict Biscop and Bede

Benedict Biscop, another well born Northumbrian, left home and went to Rome to discover the best religious rule to introduce in England. He escorted Theodore and Hadrian to England, and stayed for two years at Canterbury. With the help o

King Ecgfrith he established a monastery at Monkwearmouth in 674, and a sister foundation at Jarrow in 685. This was almost a branch of Canterbury. There were fine buildings, and Benedict brought from Rome many relics, ornaments and books. John, the chanter of St Peter's, Rome, was brought over to teach singing. The rule was strict Benedictine with stress on stability, moderation and learning. Jarrow was the residence of Bede for the greater part of his life.

Benedict's books helped to provide the material for his great work, 'The Ecclesiastical History', and here it is necessary to give some assessment of it. There is nothing else of its historical quality during the Anglo-Saxon period, and it compares favourably with the work of the greatest historians of any time. It is not merely the evidence he had at his disposal, but the sensible quality of his assessments. Although a religious historian and writing in a period of great Christian enthusiasm, he never gets carried away completely. He is able to appreciate even when he disapproves. His work shows careful collection of material and it is very well written. He even adds a chronological summary together with a brief note about the author. To him we owe the establishment of Christian dating.

"With God's help, I, Bede, the servant of Christ and priest of the monastery of the blessed Apostles Peter and Paul at Wearmouth and Jarrow, have assembled these facts about the history of the Church in Britain, and of the Church of the English in particular, so far as I have been able to ascertain them from ancient documents, from the traditions of our forebears, and from my own personal knowledge.

"I was born on the lands of this monastery, and on reaching seven years of age, my family entrusted me first to the most reverend Abbot Benedict, and later to Abbot Ceolfrid for my education. I have spent all the remainder of my life in this monastery, and devoted myself entirely to the study of the scriptures. And while I have observed the regular discipline and sung the choir offices daily in church, my chief delight has always been in study, teaching and writing.

"I was ordained deacon at the age of nineteen, and priest at the age of thirty, receiving both these orders at the hands of the most reverend Bishop John at the direction of Abbot Ceolfrid. From the time of my receiving the priesthood until my fifty-ninth year, I have worked both for my own benefit and that of my brethren, to compile short extracts from the works of the venerable Fathers on holy scripture, and to comment on their meaning and interpretation."

He then adds a list of his works. He lived from 673 to 735, mainly in his monastery at Monkwearmouth and Jarrow. York and Lindisfarne were probably the limits of his travel. It seems he kept the Canonical Hours regularly as boy, deacon and priest for 55 years. An educational centre like Jarrow received many visitors, and it could be regarded as the University of the North. One of Bede's scholars, Cuthbert by name, gives an account of his last days.

"He gave daily lessons to us his students and spent the rest of the day singing the psalms so far as his strengthen allowed. He was told that the final chapter of a book he was dictating was unfinished. So he continued. Then the same lad, named Wilbert, said again, 'Dear Master, there is one sentence still unfinished.' So he continued. Then the same lad, named Wilbert, said again, 'Dear Master, there is one sentence still unfinished.' 'Very well,' he replied, 'Write it down.' After a short while the lad said, 'Now it is finished.' 'You have spoken truly,' he said, 'It is well finished...'."

His work is his best memorial, and he deserves the title of 'The Father of English History'. For once there is great light on the North and on the Tyne in particular. Besides writing his history of the Church, Bede wrote the 'Lives of the Abbots' and a biography of Cuthbert. Here again he shows the great care he took to ascertain his facts. *"I have written nothing about the saint without first subjecting the facts to the most thorough scrutiny and have passed on nothing to be transcribed for general reading that has not been obtained by rigorous examination of trustworthy witnesses."* And yet the work is very readable.

His purpose was to strengthen faith. *"If history relates good things of good men, the attentive hearer is excited to imitate that which is good."* It is interesting to notice the word 'hearer' and not 'reader'. Readers would be limited in numbers, especially since the language of Bede's History was Latin. But it provided a compendium of information on the Sixth Age of the World. It could be used by scholars throughout Europe. One has to remember that Latin was the medium of correspondence and scholarship. There were different languages among the English as well as the Celts. *"The wealth of Northumbrian Christianity came from its fusion of the Roman and the Celtic traditions, and nowhere were the two more happily blended than in the generous mind of Bede."*

Bede's scholarship and learning continued through Egbert, his pupil at York and from Egbert to Alcuin, a scholar called to the court of Charlemagne.

An interesting example of the contacts between Northumbria and the continent is a letter of Cuthbert, Abbot of Wearmouth and pupil of Bede, to Lul, Bishop of Mainz, written in 764.

"To the most desired and sweetest friend in the love of Christ, and dearest of all prelates, Bishop Lul, Cuthbert, disciple of the priest Bede, sends greeting.

I have gratefully received the gifts of your love, and the more gratefully, in that I know you send them with the deepest affection and devotion; you have sent, namely an all silk robe for the relics of Bede, our master of blessed memory, in remembrance and veneration of him. And it indeed seems right to me, that the whole race of the English in all provinces wherever they are found, should give thanks to God, that he has granted to them so wonderful a man in their nation, endowed with diverse gifts, and so assiduous in the exercise of those gifts, and likewise living a good life; for I, reared at his feet, have learnt by experience this which I relate. And also you have sent to me for myself a multi-coloured coverlet to protect my body from the cold. This I have given with great joy to Almighty God and the blessed Apostle Paul, to clothe the altar which is consecrated to God in his church, because I have lived in this monastery under his protection for forty-six years.

Now truly, since you have asked for some of the works of the blessed father, for your love I have prepared what I could, with my pupils, according to our capacity. I have sent in accordance with your wishes the books about the man of God, Cuthbert, composed in verse and prose. And if I could have done more, I would gladly have done so. For the conditions of the past winter oppressed the island of our race very horribly with cold and ice and long and widespread storms of wind and rain, so that the hand of the scribe was hindered from producing a great number of books.

And six years ago I sent you, my brother, some small gifts, namely twenty knives and a robe made of otter-skins, by my priest Hunwine, when he was travelling to your districts and anxious to see Rome; but this priest Hunwine, arriving at the city called Beneventum, migrated from this light there. Therefore neither through him nor any of your people has any reply ever been given me whether those things reached you. We took care to send you, Father, two palls of subtle workmanship, one white, the other coloured, along with the books, and a bell such as I had by me.

And I pray that you will not spurn my petition and my need; if there is any man in your diocese who can make vessels of glass well, that you will deign to send him to me when time is favourable. But if perhaps he is beyond your boundaries outside your diocese in the power of some other, I ask your brotherly kindness to urge him to come here to us, because we are ignorant and destitute of that art. And if perchance it happen that one of the makers of glass is permitted God willing by your good offices to come to us, I will treat him with kind indulgence as long as I live. It would delight me also to have a harpist who could play on the harp which we call 'rottae'; for I have a harp and am without a player. If it be not a trouble, send one also to my disposal. I beg that you will not scorn my request nor think it laughable.

Concerning the works of Bede of blessed memory, of which you have no copies, I promise to assist your wishes, if we live.

Abbot Cuthbert greets you again and again. May Almighty God keep you safe for ever."

Bede in a letter to Egbert, Archbishop of York in 734, may have given too gloomy a picture. He took it upon himself to advise his former pupils – even to an Archbishop *"restrain yourself with pontifical dignity from idle conversations..."* He urged him to make certain that priests and teachers were sent to the remotest villages. Everyone ought to know at least the Creed and the Lord's Prayer in English. He was critical of certain monasteries that were established for improper purposes – to avoid duties to both God and King *"henceforward free from divine as well as from human service."* The country could be faced with *"the dwindling of the supply of secular troops... a lack of men to defend our territories against barbarian invasion."* There was no compensating service to God. Correspondence between men of the Church within England and with the continent, show that a good deal of creative work did take place.

Part of the cross-shaft Spital, near Hexham.

THE POLITICAL SITUATION

It is necessary briefly to return to the politics of the eighth century. The devastation of wars and dynastic changes can be exaggerated. It would be hard to imagine the artistic and literary development of the period from the Anglo-Saxon Chronicle. One wonders how far the fortuitous evidence available can affect the balanced interpretation of a period or era. This is especially felt after Bede (673–735). He wrote of his own last years: *"Both the outset and course of Ceolwulf's reign were filled with so many serious disturbances that it is quite impossible to know what to write about them."* This too could be an apology for the historian of our time.

Oswiu had helped to bring about the victory of Rome in matters religious. He, himself, in 654 had defeated Penda of Mercia, and emerged as Bretwalda. The Welsh were driven back, and he was overlord of the English kings south of the Humber. This was a critical point in the affairs of Northumbria, because Oswiu tended to look northwards instead of concentrating on the mastery of the southern kingdoms. There was, at this stage, a possibility of uniting England, but he turned his attention to the Picts, enabling Mercia, under Wulfhere, to recover. The common factors of Christianity and family relationships did not prevent the bitterest feuds. Oswiu had been brought up among the Scots of Dalriada, and his brother Eanfrith established a line of Pictish Kings. He was stirred to military activities north of the Forth. It is not certain how extensive his conquests were. Part at least of Southern Pictland was subdued, and his overlordship accepted. In 674 Ecgfrith, Oswiu's successor, had to face an invasion from Wulfhere of Mercia – this was defeated, and Mercia was laid under tribute. Wulfhere died soon afterwards, but his brother Aethelred defeated Ecgfrith in 679, thus regaining independence.

In this battle by the Trent, Aelfwine, brother of Ecgfrith, was slain. Normally this might have led to a blood-feud between the two families, but Christianity, in the person of Theodore, exercised a reconciling influence. Ecgfrith lost control of Mercia, but he gained compensation for his brother's death. Bede wrote: *"the life of no man perished for the death of that the king's brother, but only a due amercement of money was given to the king that was the avenger."* The Kings accepted the boundary of the Humber, and remained at peace with each other.

Ecgfrith had to face a rebellion in Southern Scotland, but crushed it and established his overlordship in these areas. This shows the difficulty of having to fight on two fronts. After a naval attack on Meath, he unwisely invaded Pictland, and penetrated too far. In 685 he was defeated and killed at Nechtanesmere by Brude, son of Bile. This meant the end of attempts to conquer the lands beyond the Clyde.

Aldfrith (the Learned) enjoyed a comparatively peaceful reign, 685–704. Better relations were brought about with the Picts through Christianity and their acceptance of Easter in the Roman fashion. The Picts were prepared to accept the rough boundary of the Antonine Wall, and the size of Strathclyde depended on the relative power of kings in that area.

"Northumbrian history in the eighth century provides the classic example of the way in which dynastic strife could affect the stability of an Anglo-Saxon kingdom." It was not only the rivalry of the old Deiran and Bernician houses, but also noble families were prepared to assert their claims. A great deal depended on the strength and determination of the king. When Aldfrith died in 705, he was succeeded by a seven year old son, Osred, and there was civil war for a time. 716: *"In this year Osred, King of Northumbria, was killed south of the border."* The border was the Humber distinctly recognised at that date. Osred, a wild and sacrilegious youth little lamented, was followed by Coenred for two years and Osric for eleven years. *"In this year (720) Osric, King of Northumbria, was slain and Ceolwulf succeeded to the kingdom and ruled eight years."* His descent from Ida is quoted: to him Bede dedicated his History.

In 738 Eadberht became king, and ruled 21 years. Thus he prevented further decay of the kingdom. His brother Egbert became Archbishop of York. Eadberht resumed the attempt to secure further territory from Strathclyde. He conquered Ayrshire and besieged Dumbarton, but suffered severe losses on his return. Strathclyde recovered its lost lands.

In 757 Eadberht received the tonsure, and Oswulf, his son, succeeded him. He reigned one year, *"and the members of his household killed him on July 24."* This contrasts with a story told in the Anglo-Saxon Chronicle about King Cynewulf of Wessex, who was killed while visiting a mistress in her bower. His thegns refused to take service of his killer, a prince, and killed him. In 755 Aethelbald of Mercia was murdered at Seckington, near Tamworth (the Mercian capital); so that in three years the Kings of Northumbria, Mercia and Wessex all perished at the hands of some of their own people.

In Mercia, Offa succeeded Aethelbald, and he was to make himself the most powerful ruler in the country, establishing Mercian supremacy. He was responsible for a great dyke to keep back the Welsh.

In Northumbria the sorry story of feuds continued; the new king was Aethelwald Moll, whose strength lay in Deira. The Anglo-Saxon Chronicle records that in 761 *"Moll, the Northumbrian King, slew Oswine at Aedwinselif on August 6."*

He abdicated after a reign of six years, and was succeeded by Alhred. In 774 *"the Northumbrians expelled their king, Alhred from York at Eastertide, and took Aethelred, son of Moll, as their lord and he reigned four years."* Alhred went to the Picts.

In 778 *"Aethelbald and Heardberht slew three 'high reeves'* (i.e. officials in charge of royal estates) *on 22 March... And then Aelfwald succeeded to the kingdom, and drove Aethelred out of the country, and he reigned ten years."* He was a just and pious king — the last Northumbrian King admired by any ancient writer.

In the following year the Northumbrian 'high reeves' burnt Beom the ealdorman (alderman) to death in Seletun on the 24 December.

There was mortality in the Church – Aethebert of York died, and so did Eahlmund, Bishop of Hexham; Cynewulf of Lindisfarne resigned and died later.

In 789 King Aelfwald was slain by Sicga, *"and a light was frequently seen in the sky where he was slain."* He was buried at Hexham by the church, and his nephew, Osred, son of Alhred, succeeded him, but within a year he was betrayed and driven out. Aethelred, son of Aethelwald Moll, became king again, and drowned the young sons of Aelfwald. He shewed himself without mercy, and Osred, who returned from exile, was seized and slain *"and his body lies at Tynemouth."*

In this same year King Aethelred was married for a second time to the lady Aelfled – Offa's daughter, perhaps indicating dependence. His reign did not last, for in 794 he *"was killed by his own court on April 19."* He may have deserved this, but it gave Northumbria a bad reputation. Offa, himself, was closely connected with the continent, and had dealings with Charlemagne's court. Alcuin, a scholar of York, had gone there, and through him much was known about Northumbrian affairs. When he heard of Aethelred's murder, Charlemagne denounced the Northumbrians as traitors and murderers, worse than heathen.

But Eardwulf, the next king, accepted Charlemagne's protection. He was powerful enough to challenge Cenwulf of Mercia in 801, but the Church restored peace between them. When Eardwulf was driven from his kingdom he was protected by Charlemagne, and went to his Court. He was able to return with the authority of the Pope, and reigned till 810. His son, Eanred, kept control for some thirty years, and there is little mentioned about him except his submission to Egbert of Wessex, who challenged Mercian supremacy and became Bretwalda. In 827 *"This Egbert led his levies to Dore against the Northumbrians, where they offered his submission: thereupon they parted."* This may give an impression of weakness, but Northumbria was still an important state. *"The continuity of Northumbrian scholarship, like the integrity of the Northumbrian kingdom, had survived half a century of dynastic revolutions."*

PLACES TO VISIT, WITH ANGLO-SAXON ART AND ARCHITECTURE

St Cuthbert and Durham.

Christianity in the Anglo-Saxon period is essentially expressed in the spirit and achievements of two saints – Cuthbert and Bede, different in character and contribution. At Durham Cathedral, which celebrated its 900th year last year, 1993, their gravestones will be witnessed by many people – Cuthbert at the East end and Bede at the West end. Bede's bones were transferred from Jarrow.

Cuthbert lived as a shepherd boy in the Lammermuir Hills, enjoying life, but received a call to join the religious community at Melrose, where he worked till 660 A.D. Then he went with Abbot Eata to found a monastery at Ripon. When he returned, he became Prior of Melrose and spent his time as a missionary carrying the Gospel to the lonely hills and as far away as the Solway. He was not confined to one place and visited Abbess Ebba at Coldingham. On another occasion he met the Abbess of Whitby at Coquet Island. They sought his spiritual advice. Cuthbert became Abbot of Lindisfarne and established a retreat for himself on the Farne Isles. He died there in 687 and was buried at Lindisfarne. In 698 when his body was transferred to another shrine, it was found to be incorrupt and so became an object of special veneration.

After the Danish raids in 875, several monks carried Cuthbert's coffin and relics away. In eight years they travelled in SouthWest Scotland, Cumbria and Yorkshire before halting at Chester-le-Street. King Aethelstan made special gifts to them – a stole, a maniple (an ornamental band worn on the left arm by the celebrant at the Eucharist), a girdle and a book. Cuthbert was moved again in 995, but the coffin could not be moved beyond Durham, which became the place of a cathedral and his permanent abode. Many churches were dedicated to him, but in 1069, when the Normans were ravaging the North, he was moved again to Jarrow, Bedlington Tuggal and Lindisfarne. Eventually, however, the Bishop of Durham became the most powerful figure in the North with a Palatinate or Principality. His lands outside Durham were Bedlingtonshire, Norham and Islandshire. A new monastery was built at Lindisfarne, and a church at Norham. From Crayke in Yorkshire, the Bishop could look down on York. St Cuthbert became the most popular saint in the country and pilgrims came from all parts to visit his shrine.

Battles have been fought and won under his banner. In 1104 when Cuthbert' relics were transferred to the new cathedral, they were found to be incorrupt. The survived the reformation and in 1829 were examined and reburied. Secondary relic such as cloths, vestments, portable altar and pectoral cross, together with manuscripts and the oak coffin timbers, were kept in the Cathedral Library. These can still be seen, and are regarded as the treasures of the Cathedral. There is a large collection of Anglo-Saxon crosses and carvings in the Monks' Dormitory.

The Lindisfarne Gospels are also obviously connected with Cuthbert's monastery on Lindisfarne. There is a similarity between the carvings in stone and patterns in the illuminated manuscript. Above all, the spirit of St Cuthbert is expressed in his sympathy with nature – birds, beasts, flowers and foliage. The art is of the highest quality. 83 churches are dedicated to St Cuthbert, of which 49 are in the six northern counties, but others stretch as far as Cornwall, and 17 are in Scotland. The Farne Islands, once under Cuthbert's special protection, is now a bird sanctuary under the care of the National Trust. The eider duck, affectionately known as 'Cuddy's duck', is a special reminder of the kindly saint.

The relics of St Cuthbert show that he had accepted the organisation of the Roman Church and the dignity of a bishop. He had to proceed with caution after the Synod of Whitby, since many Celtic Christians did not approve of the changes. They liked to wander, like Jesus himself, preaching and teaching, but they also wanted periods of solitude for contemplation and prayer. Cuthbert's portable altar went with him when he was on his missionary journeys. It was made of oak, carved with five crosses, covered with silver and inscribed 'in Honour of St Peter'. His pectoral cross was the sign of his faith and office. It was made of gold inset with garnets and probably of Northumbrian workmanship. His coffin was made of carved oak and has lasted some 1300 years. On the top is the figure of Christ with his hand raised in blessing. Round the sides appear the Virgin Mary with Jesus, apostles and archangels; the figures are similar to those that appear on the large stone crosses.

Lindisfarne Gospels

"Eadfrith, Bishop of the Lindisfarne Church, originally wrote this book, for God and St Cuthbert – jointly – for all the saints whose relics are in the Island. And Ethelwald, Bishop of the Lindisfarne Islanders, impressed it on the outside and covered it – as he well knew how to do. And Billfrith, the anchorite, forged the ornaments which are on it on the outside and adorned it with gold and with gems and also with gilded over silver – pure metal. And Aldred, unworthy and most miserable priest, glossed it in English between the lines with the help of God and St Cuthbert."

This was written about 950 – the Latin text was some 250 years older. Experts affirm that the Gospels were written in one hand, that of Eadfrith before he became Bishop in 698. Afterwards he would not have had time. The original cover has not survived, but that of the Gospel of St John in Cuthbert's coffin has.

Anglo-Saxon Art in Northumbria shows a number of influences.

The legacy of Rome was naturalistic and representational art. The barbarians preferred abstract design and patterns. Christianity led to the modification of native art, often a new naturalism and blend of influences. Celtic art showed a love of interlace and geometrical ornament. Anglo-Saxon art in the pagan period tended to break down forms of animal ornamentation until they became curious patterns of intertwined creatures. With the coming of Christianity there was added the decorative Mediterranean patterns such as the vine scroll and the vine inhabited by birds and beasts.

It is difficult to distinguish English and Celtic elements in the early illuminated manuscripts. They are written in an Irish hand and show a blend of elements. Manuscripts moved about a good deal and it is often impossible to determine the original home. Some experts would assign them mostly to Ireland, others to Northumbria. An Irish scribe, Ultan, was at Lindisfarne in the 7th century – writers moved about as well as their writings.

After the Synod of Whitby in 664, there was something of a Celtic retreat and Roman influences became more important. Both Wilfrid and Benedict Biscop brought back Italian books and works of art. The gospels of St Augustine were Italian. The Codex Amiatinus, now in Florence, was produced in Jarrow. However it is the Lindisfarne Gospels, from that very island, which have pride of place and remain in the British Library.

It is hard to describe them – they have to be seen and there have been numerous replicas, one of which is on display in Lindisfarne Museum. Each of the four gospels is prefaced by the figure of an evangelist with his symbol and then follows a carpet style of ornament. The first letter of each chapter is beautifully illuminated. The human figures are natural – St John in a trance and St Matthew looking to Christ for inspiration. St Mark holds a book and seems to be wondering what to write. St Luke is writing on a scroll. The ornamentation in form and colour show all the various influences aforementioned. The arcaded canon tables are included in a structure of Roman architecture with round arches. The columns are decorated with interlaced birds and beasts. The Lindisfarne Gospels have been described as *"one of the world's greatest masterpieces of manuscript painting"*. It is a miracle that they have survived a dipping in the sea, the grasping hands of Vikings and Henry VIII's seizure of monastic properties.

A visit to Lindisfarne is an interesting experience. A modern statue of St Aidan can be seen standing in an attitude of prayer between the churches. There are the regular tidal visitations, cutting the island from the mainland twice a day, and it is strange to look at the mainland from this point, to view the Farne Islands and Bamburgh's rock. We are reminded that the Anglo-Saxons were a sea-faring people and travelled a good deal in their ships. There was a monastic cell on Coquet Island and I think there would have been the landmark of a church at Newbiggin. The medieval spire tends to obscure the fact that the basis of the tower may have been Anglo-Saxon. An early church was founded here by the Lindisfarne community.

The church of St Mary on Lindisfarne is of Saxon origin, the monastery is Norman.

Churches connected with Lindisfarne

Sometimes excavation and careful scrutiny of standing masonry have shown that more survives of Saxon churches than was supposed. In 729 King Ceolwulf of Northumbria abdicated in favour of Eadbert. The Anglo-Saxon Chronicle records briefly: *"King Ceolwulf received St Peter's tonsure,"* that is he became a monk and his head was shaven in the Roman style. He was probably weary of the dangers and problems of kingship – most kings then died by the sword. Ceolwulf's life in the monastery of Lindisfarne lasted till 764, and he was buried near St Cuthbert. The monastery greatly benefited from his grants of land that would supply wealth, labour and food supplies, including fish and salt. These lands were Brainshaugh and Warkworth, Woodhorn and Whittingham, Edlingham and Eglingham, all Anglo-Saxon settlements, and it seems at each churches were established, first of timber and later of stone. The 'appurtenances' of the estates extended to Brinkburn and Rothbury and along the coast from Alnmouth to Newbiggin. So the community of St Cuthbert was greatly enriched and according to Reginald of Durham:

"On the investigation of this royal monk, the monks of the church of Lindisfarne were permitted to drink wine or beers for previously they used to drink only milk and water, according to the ancient custom of St Aidan."

Ceolwulf had a great love of the Scriptures, and Bede dedicated his 'Ecclesiastical History' to him.

At **Brainshaugh** on the river Coquet there was later established a convent and the ruins of a 12th century church remain, which now have the name of Guyzance. It is a secluded site.

Warkworth had a Saxon church and carved stones have been discovered – two headstone crosses and a round topped grave marker. The church still standing is basically Norman – a strongly built tower, and the north wall of the nave with highly placed round headed windows. The chancel consists of two bays and has reinforced rib vaulting. The church is close to the river Coquet which encloses the village on three sides, very similar to Durham.

Woodhorn, Ceolwulf's Wudcestre, has a church that appears at first not very interesting – blackened by smoke of a formerly mining area and screened by rookery trees. But closer investigation shows that the Woodhorn Church Museum possesses considerable interest. Though much restored in 1842–3, the base of the tower and west wall of the nave is 11th century. The south west corner of the narrow nave shows quoins of large irregular stones. Inside the west end of the nave, walls can be seen. The old masonry has been removed by the formation of medieval àrches on pillars. The western arches cut into Anglo-Saxon windows which are narrow and round headed, the lintel cut from a single stone. They are widely splayed, the interior opening twice as large as the exterior, seen by looking either side of the arches. The window head on the south side is curiously carved, one suggestion is for taking plaster. A further factor is that dowsing has disclosed the existence and extent of the early church – an apsidal east end is marked on the floor of the chancel, where it was excavated. While preparing the church for a museum, excavations revealed further Saxon carving, some of which was built into the walls of the church during earlier restoration. In addition to local carvings and monuments, others have been transferred from the Black Gate Museum, Newcastle upon Tyne.

First there are portions of a large upstanding carved stone cross. These crosses were the striking features of Saxon religious sites, standing to a height of 4.57m (15 ft). The arms at the top usually depict the Crucifixion, and the sides of the shaft are carved with religious scenes or naturalistic patterns. The one at Woodhorn has similar features to the Durham cross and indicates an 11th century date. The central circle and arms are decorated with interlace designs, the edges have animal patterns. Further animal patterns can be seen from a surviving panel of the shaft. Other Saxon monuments are four small upright grave markers, which carry crosses. In addition there are a number of medieval monuments, so that the church is well worth a visit. At the same time more of the Saxon atmosphere can be absorbed by going down to the sea at Newbiggin, a site well known to sailors through the ages. The sea has eroded much of the headland, but there was a Viking grave on the Cambois side of the Wansbeck. The new edition of Pevsner (1992) gives this information on Newbiggin.

"The church, particularly the interior, is archaeologically fascinating. There is no definite pre-Conquest evidence, but the long and narrow proportions of the nave and some features of the strange little unbuttressed W. tower, heavily remodelled in the 13th century, hint at early origins."

Alnmouth. Another such place is Alnmouth, which in Saxon times had the name of Twyford, where Cuthbert was chosen Bishop in 684. A cross shaft was found in 1789 near the ruins of the old church, commonly called *"Woden's church at Alemouth"*.

Alnmouth had been a prosperous port until 1806, when the river and sea breached the dunes and the site of the old church was cut off from the settlement. By this time the graveyard was being eroded and burials were transferred to Lesbury.

One side of the cross shows the Crucifixion in the centre. The sun and moon are above, thieves alongside and soldiers below with a panel of interlace. The narrow side has interlace and inscriptions. The other broad side has interlace and an inscription which runs *'Myredah meh worthe'*, i.e. *'Myredah made me'*. The name is Irish and the date probably 9th century. It is now in the Museum of Antiquities, Newcastle.

Whittingham. Some 10 miles inland and on the river Aln near the Roman road, 'Devil's Causeway', is the village of Whittingham. It has an important Saxon church, marred, however, by unsympathetic Victorian restoration. The tower was demolished halfway and rebuilt with curious pinnacles on each corner. The west wall with Saxon tower arch remained, but the Saxon type windows in the upper nave were 'gothicized'. The lower part of the tower provides an interesting architectural study.

"The quoins are the best in the county. They are long and short work, a style not found elsewhere in Northumberland and not normally associated with the North." Pevsner.

Experts consider there are two stages of building in the tower. Some of the stones are very large.

Edlingham. A few miles south is Edlingham, by name another Old English settlement. The church is a plain moorland stone structure, basically Norman, but having a square tower added in the 14th century for defensive purposes. It is quite a contrast with Whittingham. One carved stone within the church is a pre-conquest cross shaft with vine scroll and another cross slab with cross in relief. The nave has some very large long stones in the south west quoins that are also considered pre-Conquest.

Rothbury. Our route now leads us to Rothbury, the meeting centre of Upper Coquetdale, and in Saxon times it had a monastery, which seems to have been similar to Jarrow. There were two churches, connected by a central tower. An old painting shows the eastern church which was Saxon in structure and a tall tower like Whittingham, with an arch showing that here was a transept or porticus. Wallis, *c.*1767 recorded that the church was 36.57m (40 yards) long to the west. Dowsing has indicated that there were extensive buildings to the west of the tower. There was a lot of destruction before 1850 when the church was largely rebuilt. Of the greatest interest is the font, dated 1664, supported by the base of a splendid Anglo-Saxon Cross, dating to the 8th century.

The east side shows the 'Fall of Man' with curvilinear decoration and animals in the branches. The north side shows the 'Ascension of Christ'. He is raised aloft with angels on either side and the apostles looking up from below. It is said to be the oldest carving on the subject in Britain. The west side shows 'After the Fall of Man' with similar patterns and the south side has a panel of knotwork pattern, like basket-work. The area where the font is, beneath the tower, is well lighted. Photographs of other carvings from the Cross that were discovered during the restoration of the church (1850) are on display. The stones are now in the Museum of Antiquities, Newcastle.

One panel shows the figure of Christ, front facing with a halo. He is not bearded and looks youthful and appealing. He carries a book in his left hand. There is an arch above and plants on either side. It is a most attractive picture and originally it was coloured with inset eyes. Others show crowd scenes, decoration, animals in vine scroll. The Cross shows a mixture of Mediterranean, Irish Celtic and Saxon motifs, and can be linked with the Ruthwell Cross, near Dumfries, one of the best of the period, 9th century.

It would have stood 4.57m (15 ft) high and in place of the old Market Cross at Rothbury, there was erected in 1902, a similar type of cross in memory of Lord and Lady Armstrong. It has carved panels and patterns, climbing foliage, inhabited by birds and animals – including an owl, squirrels and deer with antlers. This gives some idea of the nature of the Anglo-Saxon Cross.

The Hexham road, formerly called the Corn Road, runs south from Rothbury. It passes the entrance to **Nunnykirk** Hall, where there was a Saxon carved cross, indicating a settlement. It has recently been transferred to the Museum of Antiquities in Newcastle, where there are many other sculptures. **Hartburn** is situated on the old Roman Road, called Devil's Causeway, and the church is attractively situated. The nave has massive Pre-Conquest quoins and dowsing has indicated what the early structures may have been. A plan of the church is displayed and a useful guide available.

Another place to visit in the area is **Wallington** Hall, since here are shown some of the finest illustrations of troubled times in Northumberland. Mural paintings by William Bell Scott depict the building of the Roman Wall, which the Saxons thought to be the work of giants; St Cuthbert visited on the Farnes by King Egfrid offering a bishopric; the death of the Venerable Bede at Jarrow and the Descent of the Danes on the mouth of the Tyne.

Bolam is a village of considerable interest – once it was a town with the grant of a fair and market by Edward I. It had a church, castle and rows of 200 houses. These have now gone but the church tower has been standing for 900 years. It is late Saxon in date and one of the best of its kind. Standing 16.76m (55 ft) high, it has four storeys and the belfry openings are at the third floor stage – they were usually at the top. Bells were of the greatest importance for declaring the times of church services, but could also be used for warning of danger. From the tower much could be observed. The structure stands 4.57m (15 ft) square and has walls which are 76.20cm (30 inches) thick. It is built of stone with the quoins of large side alternate stones. A break in the masonry at the middle may indicate two periods of building. The original windows were of a single light and single stone head with wide splay inwards. The lower ones were altered in the Norman period. The belfry openings have two lights and shafts with bulbous bases. The tower arch was altered and the parapet renewed later. The quoins of the west wall of the narrow nave are Anglo-Saxon. There were further alterations in the medieval period and the dowsing plan indicates other changes.

Stamfordham is an attractive village and the church of St Mary stands high at the east end of it, overlooking the 'madfens', the marshy valley of the Pont. The proportions of the church were spoilt in the 19th century restoration, when the nave was raised too high and a lot of the old stonework was removed. However, there was a Saxon Church and the quoins can be detected at the south west corner of the nave. There is a blocked Saxon arch in the west wall of the tower, which may include original stonework. This strongly built tower has small lancets on the lower two floors and above a two light bell opening.

We are now near the 'Giant's Wall', which would appear high in Saxon times, not being much robbed of stone. But when we take a look at **Heddon-on-the-Wall** church, we can see where some of the Roman stone went. The Church of St. Andrew here was Anglo-Saxon, and at the south east corner of the nave there are very large stone quoins. The original church had an apsidal east end and the remarkable rib vaulted chancel is reckoned to be early Norman in date.

From this stage the Roman Wall continues to lie under the Military Road, but the wall ditch and vallum can be picked out on the north and south sides respectively as we travel west. It is quite an exciting experience to drive along the road and dangerous to walk on it. The Wall provides the atmosphere for the site of the battle of **Heavenfield** (634) above Chollerford, where King Oswald defeated the wild hordes of Cadwallon. A large wooden cross stands at the gate of the field of battle, where a mound indicates the line of the Wall and beyond, sheltered by trees, is the **Chapel of St Oswald**.

In Saxon times it became a gathering place, and:

"As this custom has grown, they have lately built a church on the site and made the place more sacred and esteemed than any other in the eyes of all men. This is as it should be, for as far as we know there was no symbol of the Christian faith, no church and no altar erected anywhere in the land of Bernicia until their new leader in war, inspired by his zeal for the faith set up this standard of the holy cross before doing battle with his monstrous enemy." (Bede)

Since that time stone churches have been built here. The sundial gives the date of one restoration 1735, and the church was remodelled in 1887. Inside are fragments of a stone shaft and a Roman altar, probably used as the socket for a cross. From St Oswald there are splendid views in all directions. Hexham monks used to make a pilgrimage here on St Oswald's day (August 5).

We travel back along the line of the Wall and take the road to Ovingham on the River Tyne.

Ovingham. The church of St Mary is obviously Anglo-Saxon. It has a characteristic west tower standing to the height of 18.28m (60 ft), only the parapet being modern. It is roughly 3.96m (13 ft) square internally, with 0.91m (3 ft) thick walls, and the west wall of the nave projects 0.60m (2 ft) on either side of it. There are rough squared stones and side alternate quoins. The belfry stage is at the top of the tower, which has four double light windows, one on each face. There are smaller openings below and at 12.19m (40 ft) high, a doorway led into the roof of the nave. The tower arch was altered later, and in the 13th century the church was much changed with a long chancel and transepts with long lancet windows. Bewick went to school and was buried here. There are fragments of two Saxon crosses – one interlace and the other a hunting scene, which he would doubtless appreciate.

From Ovingham, the way is to Bywell, a village with two churches both of Saxon origin, and later belonging to two different baronies and monasteries. As late as 1570 it was a busy town with some 15 shops with craftsmen involved in all kinds of ironwork. But there was decay, the 1771 Flood swept many houses away and later villagers were transferred to Stocksfield. Now there is the castle, the hall and the two churches.

Bywell St Peter was a large Saxon church where in 802 Bishop Egbert of Lindisfarne was consecrated. At first glance it may not appear to be of this date, but the north wall of the nave survives to its full height and there are four small, round headed windows still in place. The south east and north east quoins are visible with side alternate structures. The nave was longer than at present and the tower was built over part of it. There is evidence of more extensive buildings. The west parts of the chancel walls are of an early date. At the north east, parts of the chancel walls are of an early date. At the north east end of the nave where it joined the chancel can be seen the roof line of a porticus or chapel, which had doors into both chancel and nave. In the building Roman stones have been used. The Saxon windows, 6.09m (20 ft) above the floor, have single stone heads and jambs. They are widely splayed to give extra light. The inside opening is twice as wide as the external. The building was much larger than now appears, and dowsing has indicated the possibility of further structures as at Jarrow or Monkwearmouth.

St. Oswald's Church, Heavenfield.

Edlingham Church

Rothbury Saxon Cross

50

Rothbury Saxon Cross

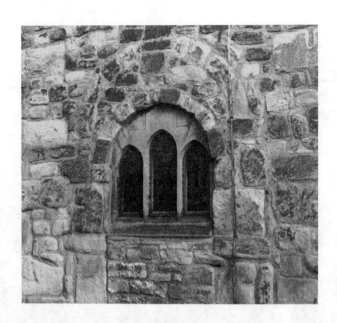

Corbridge Church : Saxon Porch

St. Mary's Church, Holy Island

Bywell St Andrew immediately attracts the eye with its splendid Saxon tower, the best in the county. It is tall, elegant and without buttresses, but with massive side alternate quoins. The belfry windows at the top stage of the tower, have double lights on each of the four sides. On the south below this stage is a high level arched doorway, while the other sides have small windows. Experts consider the lowest part may have been built in two stages as at Corbridge. The tower arch in the nave was altered during later reconstruction, much of this in the 19th century. That the church may be on the site of a pagan enclosure, is indicated by the fact that the graveyard is circular. During restoration a lot of medieval grave stones were recovered and some built into the fabric of the church. Bywell is a most interesting and beautiful place to visit.

Corbridge grew up to the east of the Roman site of Corstopitum, which was used as a stone quarry for the church and many of the houses. Here was plenty of stone already fashioned, which helped the Saxons in their early attempts to build in this material, more lasting than timber. Doors, windows, arches and columns were taken. The church of St Andrew is recorded in 786 when a bishop was consecrated here in the religious house. It probably existed a century earlier along with Bywell, Heddon and Hexham, all dedicated to St Andrew. The best approach is to view the base of the west tower, which shows its earliest part to have been a porch of Roman stone. This was later increased in height to form a tower similar to Bywell. The narrow nave of the early church can be seen and two small window arches survive in the north wall. The monastery, as it was, extended further westwards, and dowsing again indicates a complex of buildings. The elegance of the tower is rather spoilt by the structures to the north and south of the base, and the imposition of a large modern clock face – how much better to have time from bells!

Inside, the tower arch survives, fully Roman with its jambs, voussoirs and moulded imposts – 4.87m (16 ft) high and 2.43m (8 ft) wide. The original doorway to the west was blocked and a three light window inserted. The old nave walls have been detected beneath the floor. A building to the north of the tower, may have been the priest's residence, until the tower was built in the churchyard, again of Roman stone.

Corbridge has much to offer the visitor.

Wall. On the way to Hexham it is worth remembering that there is written evidence that in this area was a Saxon royal palace and a church at Wall. Here King Oswy had received King Sigberht of the East Saxons, who was baptised with his followers. In 653 A.D. Peada, son of Penda of Mercia, who married Oswy's daughter, was baptised here. The palace and church would be similar to Yeavering and near to Heavenfield, the place of Oswald's victory, accessible by Roman roads.

Hexham, near the junction of the North and South Tyne, was a Saxon bishopric and here was established the church and priory of St Andrew. The founder was Wilfrid, who won the day for Rome at the Synod of Whitby. In 674 King Ecgfrid married Etheldrid, daughter of King Ine of East Anglia. She granted extensive lands to Wilfrid, who started to build his church in Roman fashion, using stone from local Roman sites and Roman masons. From his visits to Rome he knew a lot about Roman churches and their decoration. His basilica was completed between 674 and 678. King Ecgfrid divorced his wife, who wanted to enter a nunnery. The new queen disliked Wilfrid and got him dismissed – he held York, Ripon (which he built) and Hexham. Wilfrid went again to Rome to appeal, and Eata covered Lindisfarne and Hexham, until 684 when Cuthbert became Bishop.

When Eata died St John of Beverley became Bishop of Hexham. He had a retreat at Warden, much visited by the sick and needy. Later Wilfrid was restored to Hexham and Ripon. He died in 709 and his friend Acca became bishop, following a similar policy and continuing to embellish the church. He collected books and relics (kept in the crypt) and after he died in 737, a cross was raised in his honour at Hexham, where he was buried. The cross was broken later, but most of it recovered except the top. It stood 4.26m (14 ft) high and the vine scroll pattern shows the Roman influence.

Later the church was ravaged by the Danes and the bishopric discontinued. After the Norman Conquest, Hexhamshire was acquired not by St Cuthbert of Durham, but by William, Norman Archbishop of York. An Augustinian priory was established at Hexham. It would seem that the nave of Wilfrid's church was restored and the building was extended eastwards.

There is a description which gives an idea of Wilfrid's church, at one time the finest church north of the Alps. It had crypts and oratories beneath the floor, constructed in the best stonework. The floor above had polished columns and ornate arches. The building was three storeys high with stairs, galleries and towers. Aisles and porches were on either side, with many statues and carvings. Altars were erected to the Virgin Mary, St John and other saints.

Today the most impressive part still remaining is the crypt, similar to that of Ripon, and excavations have revealed what may be a side chapel to the east of it. It is entered from the west down a flight of steps, leading to a barrel vaulted chamber 2.74m (9 ft) by 1.52m (5 ft) in area. From this, holy relics could be seen through grill in the main chamber, measuring 4.26m (14 ft) by 2.43m (8 ft). Then there was another small chamber and steps which were the way out for pilgrims. There was yet another passage reserved for the clergy. Some of the Roman stones have inscriptions and it is considered that they would have been plastered over.

Above ground some of the lower courses of the west wall are Saxon and the outer wall of the north aisle. There is an apse below the floor of the chancel, which was the east end of the church. The stone frith stool or Wilfrid's chair is now in view in the chancel as well as a small Saxon chalice. The extensive restorations in the last century, without the present day type of excavation, make the history of the priory church very difficult to interpret. There are, however, a lot of carvings and stone fragments built into the walls and in the museum. Most impressive is the monument to the Roman standard bearer of the Ala Petriana, a cavalry regiment. He is depicted in uniform on horseback, bearing his standard, and beneath him a barbarian crouches in a ditch with his sword raised. It is not clear whether Flavinus is riding down the enemy or whether the hairy man brought about his death. The stone was found beneath the passage that leads from the church to the cloister in 1881, and now stands at the bottom of the midnight stairs in the south transept. Acca's cross, a different kind of monument, stands on the other side. William of Malmesbury wrote: *"at Hexham they see the glories of Rome."*

Little did pilgrims realise that they walked over the tombstone of a Roman standard bearer and went underground to a crypt built of Roman stones – one mutilated inscription indicated that Caracalla, son of Septimius Severus, killed his brother, Geta, becoming sole Emperor of Rome in 212 A.D. He was killed in 217 and his name erased from a monument.

To the west of Hexham, where the two Tynes meet is **Warden** with a church dedicated to St Michael. It is yet another of the Tyne Valley churches with a Saxon West tower. Tall and unbuttressed, it is constructed of Roman stone with large irregular quoins and small round headed windows. The west end of the nave is of the same date. Bede wrote that here was St John of Beverley's retreat:

"There is a building in a retired situation and enclosed by a sparse wood and a trench about a mile and a half from Hexham and on the opposite side of the Tyne with an oratory dedicated to St Michael the Archangel where the man of God used frequently, as occasion offered, particularly in Lent, to reside with a few companions."

The church tower is 4.87m (16 ft) square and 13.71m (45 ft) to the top of the Saxon stage. The west wall of the nave extends 0.76m (2 ft 6 ins.) on either side. A fine tower arch measures 2.43m (8 ft) high by 1.67m (5 ft 6 ins.) wide. The imposts are moulded Roman stones. The original floors of the tower have been altered. There are Roman stones among those displayed in the porch. In the churchyard near the tower is a cross with a crudely cut hammer head, which may date from the 7th century. A large earthwork overlooks the site.

From Warden we follow the North Tyne to **Simonburn**, where the church is dedicated to St Mungo. He was also known as Kentigern, a monk of Irish traditions and mainly concerned with Cumbria and S.W. Scotland and much given to

55

travelling. At Simonburn, St Mungo's well was in the church and presumably used for baptism. Evidence of a Saxon church here is shown by a hogback stone of the 7th century, a memorial re-used in medieval times for a woman's grave. There is also part of a Saxon cross with carved patterns on each side. Dowsing indicates an early church here.

At **Birtley**, to the North, the church of St Giles contains an inscribed stone on the north wall of the chancel with a cross and letters O R P E (Pray for?). The date is about 700 A.D. and the cross bars at the end of the arms are similar to the Lindisfarne Gospels.

Bellingham church is dedicated to St Cuthbert, and there is a well where miracles occurred in Cuthbert's name. He consecrated the spring, which is now confined to a pant, from which the water flows continuously.

Corsenside, overlooking the River Rede, was also dedicated to St Cuthbert. In medieval times the church belonged to the Augustinian canonesses of **Holystone**. Their church is worth a visit, since associated with it is the Holy Well. Here Paulinus is said to have brought about the baptisms of many early Christians. Originally, the well was dedicated to St Ninian, a much travelled Scottish saint associated with Iona and particularly with Whithorn. We can imagine the route he travelled, using Roman roads. He would no doubt, visit places like Ruthwell and Bewcastle. His wells are to be found near Roman roads, including one near Whittingham. Holystone is on a Roman road leading from Rochester to Learchild. The well here was re-dedicated by the nuns to the Virgin Mary and remained a place of importance locally. In 1780 the surround to the pool was restored and a stone statue of Paulinus was brought from Alnwick and placed in the centre. Later he was transferred to the side and the mid-position taken up by a wheel cross. Lady's Well is now in the possession of the National Trust and open to visitors, who may see a supply of natural water and realise its importance to our Anglo-Saxon ancestors.

Bewcastle. The routes to S.W. Scotland followed the Roman Wall and Roman roads, hence the importance of **Bewcastle** in the north east angle of Cumbria. The church, dedicated to St Cuthbert, was built within the confines of a Roman fort. Near to the church stands the Bewcastle cross, the quality of which rivals Ruthwell. *"There is nothing as perfect as these two crosses and of a comparable date in the whole of Europe."* Pevsner.

The cross has lost its head, but still stands 4.41m (14 ft 6 ins). above the pedestal. It stood before any church was built and marked a sacred meeting place for the Celtic missionaries who travelled to and fro. Cuthbert's coffin may well have rested here for a time. The cross has been dated to the late 7th century, since an inscription in runes commemorates Alcfrith, the son of King Oswy. Oswy died in 670 A.D. but some experts think the cross is 8th century. Like Ruthwell, the interest is the sacred figures carved upon it, which carry the Christian message. The west side of the cross has, at the bottom, an arched recess within which is St John with his eagle symbol. Above this is the runic inscription and then the figure of Christ, stepping on a lion and a snake. He carries a scroll in one hand and the other is raised in blessing. Then at the top is John the Baptist carrying the Agnus Dei (Behold the Lamb of God). The south side has, from the bottom upwards, panels of knot work, vine scrolls, looser knot work, a large vine scroll with what appears to be a sundial and another knot panel. The east face has a long vine scroll, inhabited by birds and beasts. By contrast, the north face has panels of vine scroll, knot and chequer patterns with another vine scroll at the top. The use of the vine scroll decoration shows the Mediterranean influence, and it is considered that special craftsmen travelled the country to complete such works.

The **Ruthwell** cross in Dumfriesshire is very similar in size and decoration, the difference is that whereas the Bewcastle cross has weathered outside, this is within the church. Broken at the Reformation, it was recovered and restored. The arms of the cross portrayed the evangelists. There are five main panels of sculpture on each of the broader faces of the cross. On one side are John the Baptist, Christ in glory, Paul and Anthony, the Flight into Egypt and the Nativity: on the other can be seen the Visitation, Mary Magdalene washing Christ's feet, Christ healing a blind man, the Annunciation and the Crucifixion. There are Latin inscriptions and on the narrower faces are vine scroll ornament with birds and beasts.

There are passages from the Old English poem, the 'Dream of the Rood'. The Cross, made from a tree, is made to tell the story of Christ. He is likened to a young hero in battle with the devil and all his works.

"Then the young hero that was God Almighty,
stripped himself strong and steadfast.
Bold in the sight of many,
He mounted the high cross when he would redeem mankind.
I trembled as he clasped me,
Yet I durst not bow to the ground.
I was raised up as a cross. I bore the noble King,
The Lord of the heavens, I dared not bend.
They mocked us both together, I was all soaked in blood,
Streaming from the man's side, when he had sent forth his spirit.
They bewailed the King's death. Christ was on the cross.

The eager ones came there from afar
To that Prince. I beheld all that.
I was bitterly grieved with sorrows, but bowed to the hands of men,
Standing bespattered with blood; I was utterly wounded with spears.
Then they laid down the limb-weary one, stood at the head of his body,
Then they looked at heaven's lord, and he rested himself there a whole."

It is one of the most moving poems in the English language and combines with one of the greatest works of art.

After Bewcastle we return to the mouth of the Tyne. The old name for **Tynemouth** was Benebalcrag and that of Newcastle was Monkchester. South of the river was South Shields where a monastery of St Hilda was being built. There was stone almost on site, but timber had to be brought down the river. We are told that monks on their timber rafts were in danger of being blown out to sea with little concern from some of the locals. However young Cuthbert was there and called on them to pray with him and remarkably the wind changed and the monks were saved. This incident was remembered later.

A monastery was established at Tynemouth in the 8th century, and it was to become a well-known landmark. Osred, son of Alhred, was killed on his return from exile and buried here in 792. A series of kings were exiled or assassinated and the decline of the kingdom had set in.

In 793 worse happened – the Danes attacked Lindisfarne and in 794 Jarrow suffered. Tynemouth was attacked in 800 and later in 875 the monastery was burnt. Little more is recorded about it, but some church must have continued there, for in 1065 a priest, Edmund, had a vision of St Oswin, who was killed by his rival Oswy and buried there. After some difficulty a coffin, said to be Oswin's, was discovered. The presence of a saint was of the greatest importance to the Norman monastery that was built here. A number of Anglo-Saxon remains of crosses and carved shafts have been discovered, and can be seen in the Museum of Antiquities, Newcastle.

The **Museum of Antiquities** in the University of Newcastle, has a fine collection of Roman antiquities – altars, inscriptions, pottery, armour, models of forts and the Roman Wall. The Saxons used Roman stone and Roman methods of building. The style of architecture is called Romanesque.

There are Saxon artifacts on display and others in stone. Cinerary urns were used by the Saxons before they became Christian and later Christian burials were recorded by carved stones and small crosses. A number of grave markers, including the piece of the Falstone cross, are on display. Beads, brooches and sleeve-clasps are shown, and nearby are Viking weapons of war.

The Nunnykirk cross and parts of those from Rothbury and Alnmouth can be seen. A catalogue has been compiled of the Anglo-Saxon exhibits, and the Capheaton bowl which was hung from a tripod, is very interesting. No one is certain about its purpose. The Museum has a facsimile of the Lindisfarne Gospels and the Franks Casket, a whalebone box of about 700 A.D. which was carved in Northumbria. It is a unique survival of secular art with a variety of Christian, classical and pagan scenes. It can be used to illustrate the life of the times, including warfare, and it depicts a siege with helmeted cavalrymen and archers. One side of the front panel shows the Adoration of the Magi, and on the other Weland the Smith takes vengeance on his enemies. The runic inscription can be translated:

"This is the whale's bone. The sea cast up the fish on the rocky shore.
The ocean became turbid where he swam round on the shingle."

The Saxons called the sea 'the whale's path'.

Jarrow. By 685 the church here was completed and Jarrow, with Monkwearmouth, became one monastery in two places. Jarrow was famous for its crafts and for the works of Bede. It was sacked by the Vikings in 794, but grave crosses and covers indicate that some religious life continued. In the 11th century, Bede's bones were stolen and taken to Durham. Later Jarrow became a cell of Durham, and in time some of the buildings became ruinous.

In 1782 the nave, or the west church (St Paul's) had to be rebuilt. Investigations have shown that the Saxon church had a long narrow nave with a north aisle and, to the south, four porticus. It also had a square ended chancel. There was a gap with a porch connecting it with the present chancel, which was the eastern Saxon church (St Mary's). Later a tower had been built over the gap between the two churches.

The east church of St Mary which retains much of the old structure, measures 4.57m (15 ft) wide within the walls and is 12.19m (40 ft) long. Hutchinson (1787) wrote that the west church measured 27.43m (90 ft) by 5.79m (19 ft). The east church was built from Roman stone and the quoins of massive side alternative construction. Three windows with monolithic rounded heads survive in the south wall, but none have survived in the north wall. There is evidence that these windows had glass in Saxon times.

In excavations a number of carved and ornamental stones have been recovered. Some remain in the church, but others are in the museum. The foundation stone of 685 is re-positioned on the wall of the church. The lower stages of the tower are of Saxon construction.

Jarrow–Monkwearmouth, in its time, was a very large monastery, and the number of 600 inmates has been mentioned; so in addition to the churches there would be other extensive buildings. Both monastic sites are near rivers and, on sloping ground to the south, other buildings were erected. None of these remain above ground in modern times, but excavations have revealed their presence – some 15.24m (50 ft) south of the church and built of stone. One measuring 27.88m (91 ft 6 ins.) by 7.92m (26 ft) has been termed the Refectory. An annexe was added to the south.

Another building to the east of it measured 18.28m (60 ft) by 7.92m (26 ft) and was divided into three apartments, one large and two smaller. This has been considered to be the Chapter House. Both buildings had glass in the windows and plastered walls. They were destroyed by fire, and the other structures were interpreted as huts for residence and workshops, especially for metal and glass making. Evidence has emerged of agriculture on the site and fishing, very important for the monks.

Jarrow Hall, a late 18th century mansion, has become the Bede Monastery Museum. It is a place for housing religious relics and an interpretation centre for both the Saxon and medieval monasteries. A good deal of the window glass has been framed, showing its quality.

The museum has a regular programme of arts and crafts exhibitions, which relate to the work of the former monastery – for example artwork and calligraphy. From time to time feasts and mock Viking and Anglo-Saxon combats are held. During the next few years, several acres of adjacent land will be converted to an Anglo-Saxon landscape with fields, ploughing, reconstructed timber buildings for homes, crafts and animals. You are called upon to 'enjoy the unique experience of rediscovering the world of the Venerable Bede.'

With this in mind we might remember the story that Bede tells about Caedmon, a herdsman attached to the Abbey of Whitby. It was the custom of villagers in the evening to play the harp and take turns in singing or telling a story, while eating and drinking. When the harp approached Caedmon, he panicked and went out. He lay down to sleep with his cattle, and as he dreamed someone stood by him and said, *"Caedmon, sing me something."* He replied, *"I could not sing and for this reason I left the banquet and retired hither, because I could not sing."* The stranger said that he must sing – *"Sing the beginning of Creation."* It was the call of God, and Caedmon began to praise the Creator and all creation. When he awakened he remembered what he had sung and added more to it. This attracted the attention of the abbess, who persuaded him to become a monk. Not much of his work has survived, but he inspired others.

Caedmon's Hymn

Now must we hymn the Master of Heaven
The might of the Maker, the deeds of the Father
The thought of his heart. He, Lord everlasting
Established of old the source of all wonders:
Creator all-holy, He hung the bright heaven,
A roof high upreared, o'er the children of men;
The King of mankind then created for mortals
The world in its beauty, the earth spread beneath them,
He, Lord everlasting, omnipotent God.

Monkwearmouth. Monkwearmouth is very similar to Jarrow, for which it was the model. Both sites in modern times have been crowded by housing and industrialisation, and both had access to rivers.

Here also there were originally two Saxon churches – St Peter and St Mary. The difference is that Monkwearmouth has a tall tower at the west end, Anglo-Saxon in date and of two periods. Originally it had two storeys and four doors, the north and south doors leading into a porticus. Above the second string course a tower was erected of three more storeys – the belfry stage being at the top with double windows. The quoins or corner stones of both the tower and west wall of the nave are side alternate. Other windows in the tower are single round headed in structure. The doorway of the porch bears evidence of the intricate workmanship of the original building. There are entwined birds' heads and lathe turned balusters on either side. The same high quality is seen in the glass fragments that were recovered from excavations and put on display with other exhibits within the church. The walls, like Jarrow, were decorated with painted plaster and a cement floor with rushed tiles, made in the Roman fashion. The two churches were later embodied in a larger medieval church. The Saxon St Peter's had side chapels.

In the 19th century, and during later excavations, much sculpture with grave stones was found, since there was a large cemetery on the site. There were foundations of other buildings to the south of the church, including what has been interpreted as a covered corridor. We know from Bede that dormitories and other buildings were set up, but they were disturbed and built over at a later stage. The monastery was severely damaged in Danish raids and for a time the monks lived in huts. The church is still in use – the church of St Peter is the nave and that of St Mary is the chancel with additions.

It has been said that Monkwearmouth and Jarrow have produced more early medieval glass than anywhere else in the West.

Escomb, St John the Evangelist. Pevsner wrote that this was *"one of the most important and moving survivals of the architecture of the time of Bede and one of the only three complete Saxon churches surviving in Britain."*

It is considered to have been set up, as Bede said, on the estate of a nobleman. The site probably had previous religious associations since the graveyard is circular, on a knoll, overlooking lower ground. Mining developed about it, making the church look a little gloomy since the stone has been smoke-blackened. The interior has been whitewashed, a practice disapproved by some, but others have pointed out that the interiors of Jarrow and Monkwearmouth were plastered. This, together with small but widely splayed windows, gives much more light than might be supposed.

The stonework for building the church came from the Roman fort at Binchester, and the chancel arch, as at Corbridge, may have been a straight transfer. The church has a long, tall, narrow nave measuring 13.25m (43 ft 6 ins) by 4.41m (14 ft. 6 ins). The walls stand 6.70m (22 ft) high, and the window sills are 3.96m (13 ft) from the ground. Between two original windows on the south edge is a Saxon sundial. Excavations have shown that there was a western annexe and a porticus on the north. Window glass was found and some stone carvings. The quoins of the nave are described as side alternate. The chancel is 3.04m (10 ft) square and the chancel arch is 4.57m (15 ft) high and 1.52m (5 ft) wide. Altogether it is a most interesting church to visit, and perhaps more than any other recalls the Anglo-Saxon past.

"after Durham Cathedral, the most impressive ecclesiastical building in the county." (Collins Guide to English Parish Churches, 1958).

About three miles south of Escomb is **South Church, St Andrew, Auckland.**

This contains a very good example of a 8th–9th century Saxon cross, assembled from pieces, which now stands within the church at the west end. It is similar in design to Bewcastle and Ruthwell. There is a Crucifixion scene and inhabited vine scroll with birds and animals. An archer is shown shooting at birds and animals. The base is carved with three-quarter length figures. The church also possesses a 10th–11th century grave marker.

Further south still on the Roman road, called Dere Street, is a standing stone which was probably an estate marker of the village of **Bolam**. It is called **Legs Cross**, and consists of part of a cross shaft and socket from about 650 A.D., now making an interesting landmark. Next on Dere Street is Piercebridge, the site of a Roman bridge, fort and settlement.

Staindrop, now a market town, was in 1020 an estate granted to St Cuthbert by King Canute, Danish ruler of All-England. The present church, dedicated to S

Mary, has a lengthy history, which is enshrined in the fabric. The earliest Saxon church in stone had chancel and nave, which was later extended and a West tower added. The walling can be seen above the chancel arch and in the nave above the arcades where there are small splayed windows. There may have been side chapels covered by later aisles, which extend over the north and south face of the tower. The upper part is of later date, but the Saxon quoins can still be seen. A 9th century cross shaft has been built into a north west buttress and a sundial above the chancel arch.

Aycliffe. At Aycliffe St Andrew part of the nave walls are Saxon. The west quoins of a 10th century nave can be seen within the church. Like Staindrop, it was an estate centre. There are numerous fragments of Saxon sculpture, including two incomplete 10th century cross shafts, one with a crucifixion scene and the other interlaced with animals.

Leighington. The church of St Michael has Saxon walling of an aisleless nave and chancel with possibly a west tower. It was much extended in the Norman period.

At **Sockburn**, the church of All Saints stands close to the hall. The estate was given to the Community of St Cuthbert about 990 A.D. It later became the parish church. There are fragments of a 10th–11th century Saxon nave with massive side alternate quoins. Excavations revealed an early chancel, but most important was the collection of crosses and hog-back grave covers that have been put on display. The hog-backs show animals, birds and hunting scenes – men on horseback with spears. Cross shafts also show spearmen, birds and a drinking horn, described as 'distinctly Scandinavian in style'. The church may have become the central church of a Viking estate.

Norton is near to Stockton-on-Tees but preserves its identity. The church, dedicated to St Mary the Virgin, is Saxon in date and cruciform in shape with a central crossing tower, making it unusual. The 10th century tower is in good condition, but the battlements are modern. Pevsner wrote:

"One of the most rewarding village churches in County Durham, owing to the most complete survival of its Saxon crossing tower."

The north transept, side walls of the south transept and vestiges of nave and chancel of the Saxon church still remain. There seems to have been a wooden gallery round the inside of the tower with doors giving access to the upper parts of nave, transepts and chancel. Above this level small windows in the tower provide the necessary light. The Saxon masonry probably dates from the 10th century. Much of the fabric of the nave is Saxon and scars on the tower walls indicate the steeply pitched roof over the narrow nave. Within the church are some cross shaft fragments. Recently some 80 burials have been uncovered in a Saxon cemetery here.

Billingham is a name that makes one think of the giant ICI company and its noxious vapours. The church of St Cuthbert, however, is a pleasant surprise. An early church was built by Bishop Ecgred of Lindisfarne (830–45), but it may have been a rebuilding after Viking raids. The church was a minster of a large estate. The magnificent west tower was added to an existing church about 1000 A.D. The lower 0.69m (20 ft) of the east wall of the tower belong to the west wall of the nave, or which the north and south walls still exist, pierced by Norman arcades. The doorway from nave to tower has a semi-circular tympanum. The tower now stands 18.28m (60 ft) high – 16.45m (54 ft) to the top of the original work. There is a string course at belfry level and the belfry windows are double. Some sculptured fragments of stone are built into the walls. The best piece, now in the British Museum, is an early 8th century grave marker bearing a cross, with alpha and omega and asking 'pray for our brothers and all Christian men'.

Hartlepool. Further north on the coast is Hartlepool with the church of St Hilda on the headland. The church is medieval, but this was the site of a monastery founded in 646 A.D. to accommodate, like Whitby, both monks and nuns. The most famous abbess was St Hilda, taught by St Aidan, and member of a noble family. In 657 she set up a monastery at Whitby, where the Synod was held in 663 A.D. Remains from recent excavations can be seen in the local museum.

Hart was the mother church of Hartlepool and here, at the church of St Mary Magdalene, can be seen the structure of an early Saxon building with aisleless nave and chancel. The corners of the nave are of side alternate construction. Above the present chancel arch is evidence of an earlier one. There is a small window in the north wall of the nave and a number of pre-Conquest carved stones are on display at the west end. They include several fragments of cross shafts with a horseman interlace, carved figures, a 'haloed' figure below a lamb and a winged creature with a book. The short square tower was built in Norman times and seems different in proportion to the more slender Saxon towers.

Pittington, four miles north east of Durham, belonged to the monastery of Durham in Saxon times and, though much rebuilt in Norman and Victorian times, evidence of the early church remains. The 12th century arcades cut into the small windows of the earlier nave walls – four of these have survived. They are about 4.26m (14 ft) above the floor, and inside are splayed to measure 1.21m (4 ft) wide and 2.13m

64

ft) tall. Outside they measure 1.21m (4 ft) in height, but the light opening is only 38cm (15 ins) wide. The church is now dedicated to St Laurence and the building shows the immediate influence of Durham. Some 12th century wall paintings of St Cuthbert can be related to those in the Cathedral.

Some distance away is **Seaham** on the coast, where for years coal has dominated the scene.

The church of St Mary is one of the most interesting in the county. Its age was not recognised until 1913 during repairs, when large quantities of soil were taken away. The workmanship of the nave differs from that of the chancel, rebuilt in Norman times. There are large side alternate quoins and a band of herringbone pattern masonry in the north wall. Three surviving early windows, round headed and single splayed, can still be seen. The church is very like Escomb and excavations (1913) revealed a chancel about 3.04m (10 ft) square internally, showing both churches had similar dimensions. The nave of Seaham has all four quoins surviving, and the Saxon windows are wide splayed with evidence of rebates for wooden shutters. The date of the building is late 7th century and early 8th century, and Roman stones were used in construction. Did it come from **Chester-le-Street** or a site nearer the coast?

At **Chester-le-Street** there are now no visible remains of the Roman fort but the church, dedicated to St Mary and St Cuthbert, impresses with its tall and slender spire. The original church here was built of wood, said to be brought from Lindisfarne by Cuthbert's porters. It was rebuilt in stone circa 1056 A.D. by Bishop Egelric of Durham within the area of a Roman fort. Foundations of it were discovered in the Anchorage – once a hermit's cell within the walls of the church. He had a squint to see services and a slit to receive food. The Anker's House was later enlarged to accommodate four windows and now it contains a small museum, telling the history of the church.

Pilgrims revisit Durham and pass on to St Wilfrid's Ripon and York to meet the Vikings!

DURHAM

Part of cross-head at Durham.

THE VIKING PERIOD

The threat to Northumbria was not so much from Mercia or Wessex, but from the sea – the inroads of 'heathen men'. The first of these attacks is recorded in 787 on the kingdom of Wessex.

Three Norse ships approached the southern shores, and a reeve rode up asking them to go to the royal manor. He was promptly killed. *"These were the first ships of the Danes to come to England."* The Anglo-Saxon Chronicle speaks of 'the Northmen' and 'Danes' as indistinguishable terms, but they have to be differentiated. They came to these islands at different times, by different routes, and settled in different areas. The common factors were that they were Scandinavian similar in race, language and religion. The Northmen came from Norway, and tended to take the Atlantic routes – North Britain, Scotland, the Isles, the West Coast and Ireland. The Danes originated from Denmark, and moved down the Channel attacking both coasts.

The early raids in both the South and North of England appear to be Norse Their lands, limited in size, were subject to the pressure of population. There was not enough land for farming, and some took to trading. It has to be remembered that they were traders and settlers as well as pirates. The very name 'Norway' is the 'North-way' – the name given to a trade route. The word 'Viking' denotes sea warrior, and presents the picture of a ruthless plunderer. The Vikings were heathen who had a habit of burning and plundering churches. They knew that the churches had valuables, but only gold, silver and jewellery appealed to them. They were lacking in any kind of restraint, and were prompt to fight each other.

Their longships were superior to anything else at the time. They also used fortified bases or forts, and were quick in movement. They were well armed with helmets and shirts of mail. Kite-shaped shields were carried and long-handled battle axes. Their hefty iron ware, now reposing in museums, is very impressive, and their visitations always increased the death-rate. Added to the Litany were the words *"From the fury of the Northmen, Good Lord deliver us."*

The early raids on Northumbria were probably by Norsemen on the western route. In 793 the Anglo-Saxon Chronicle recalls that *"terrible portents appeared over Northumbria and miserably frightened the inhabitants: these were exceptional flashes of lightning and fiery dragons were seen flying in the air. A great famine soon followed these signs, and a little after that in the same year on the 8th of January* (probably a mistake for June) *the harrying of the heathen miserably destroyed God's church in Lindisfarne by rapine and slaughter."*

In the same year Alcuin wrote a letter to Ethelred, King of Northumbria: *"Lo it is nearly 350 years that we and our fathers have inhabited this most lovely land and never before has such terror appeared in Britain as we have now suffered from a pagan race, nor was it thought that such an inroad from the sea could be made. Behold the Church of St Cuthbert spattered with the blood of the priests of God, despoiled of all its ornaments: a place more venerable than all in Britain is given as a prey to pagan peoples..."*

He regards this disaster as a punishment for their sins.

"... from the days of King Aelfwald fornications, adulteries and incest have poured over the land..." He condemns their luxurious ways of living. *"Consider the dress, the way of trimming the hair, the luxurious habits of the princes and the people. Look at your trimming of beard and hair, in which you have wished to resemble the pagans..."* There is the greatest contrast of rich and poor. *"...feasting like Dives clothed in purple and Lazarus dies of hunger at the gate."* His advice to them indicated the path of virtue. *"Let your use of clothes and food be moderate."*

Alcuin also sent a letter of consolation to Abbot Higbald of Lindisfarne and his monks after the raid. Brondsted in his book 'The Vikings' gives the archaeological evidence.

"While working on the restoration of Lindisfarne monastery, English archaeologists found a curious carved stone dating, apparently, from soon after the sack of the monastery, and illustrating the melancholy event. On one side of the stone were carved various symbols of Christianity – the Cross, the sun and the moon, God's hands, and worshippers at prayer. On the other hand were depicted the violators of the shrine dressed outlandishly in rough jerkins and narrow trousers, swinging their swords and battle-axes as they advanced to destruction. This Lindisfarne stone is a poignant monument, fashioned perhaps by some Anglo-Saxon monk who witnessed this early example of Viking pillage."

The tale of terror continued.

In 794 *"And Northumbria was ravaged by the heathen, and Ecgfrith's monastery at Jarrow looted: and there one of their leaders was slain and some of their ships besides were shattered by storms: and many of them were drowned there and some came ashore alive and were slain at once at the river mouth."*

The Norse raiders were mainly concerned with Scotland and Ireland, where kingdoms were established. The Danes attacked the East and South coasts of England with growing force. In 835 they devastated Sheppey, and in the following year thirty-five ships attacked. In 838 a great pirate host attacked Cornwall, and Egbert drove them off. In 840 the Danes suffered defeat at Southampton, but gained possession of Portland, and killed an ealdorman. In the following year they slew an ealdorman and many people at Romney. In 843 they defeated King Aethelwulf at Carhampton, but in 848 were defeated on the Parret in Somerset. In 851 they made several attacks – 350 ships came into the Thames and stormed London and Canterbury. Aethelwulf and his son Aethelbald defeated them at Acleah with great slaughter. But *"the heathen for the first time remained over the winter."*

The raids were becoming much more serious, and in 844 Aethelred o:
Northumbria was expelled. He may have wanted to purchase peace, and wa
replaced by Raedwulf who was prepared to fight. His coins show that his reig‹
lasted only six months, and he was killed in battle. The Danes continued to attacl‹
the lands of the English and of the Franks.

In 865 matters took a much more serious turn, when Ivar and Halfdene, sons o‹
Ragnor Lothbrok, arrived with a great host in East Anglia. The East Angles mad‹
peace and provided the Danes with horses. In 866 the Danes attacked York, *"An‹
there was a great dissension among the people themselves; and they repudiate‹
King Osberht and accepted Aelle, a king not of royal birth: and it was late in th‹
year when they set about making war against the host, nevertheless they gathere‹
great levies and went to attack the host at York and stormed the city (March 21,
and some of them got inside and an immense slaughter was made among th‹
Northumbrians there, some inside, some outside, and both kings were slain and th‹
remnant made peace with the host."* Aelle was cruelly put to death by the sons c
Ragnar, whom he is supposed to have slain.

The Danes accepted Egbert as King, North of the Tyne, and turned to Merci‹
and East Anglia. The Abbey of Peterborough was burnt. From 870 to 871 the
fought many battles against Alfred of Wessex, but in 872 *"went the host int‹
Northumbria."* A rebellion had to be crushed, and King Egbert, who died in 87:
was replaced by Ricsige. Then Egbert II ruled beyond the Tyne.

The Danish army had divided, and Halfdene in 874 *"went with a part of th‹
host into Northumbria, and took winter quarters on the River Tyne; and the ho‹
overran that land, and made frequent raids against the Picts and against th‹
Strathclyde Britons."*

In the following year, 875, *"Halfdene shared out the lands of Northumbria an‹
they were engaged in ploughing and making a living for themselves."* The land th‹
was divided was Deira. Guthrum's host made war on Wessex and in that year tc
"Rollo invaded Normandy with his host and reigned 50 years." (Two hundred yea
later Rollo's successors ruled all England.)

By this stage the English kingdoms, with the exception of Wessex, ha
disintegrated. The Danes had occupied a great part of Mercia, and Northumbr
seems to have divided into a mainly Danish Deira and an Anglian Bernicia. Egbe
II, who reigned from 876–878, was not a puppet. The Church had been considerab‹
disrupted, and the travels of St Cuthbert's remains are symptomatic of thi
However, after the death of Halfdene in 883, he returned to Northumbria fro‹
North Britain, and obtained a resting place at Crayke. A new king, Guthred ‹
name, gave Cuthbert lands at Chester-le-Street, where he remained till his la
removal to Durham. Guthred, according to tradition, was a slave boy, probably ‹

mixed Anglo-Danish blood, who lived at Whittingham in Bernicia. His reign lasted till 895, and he was involved in conflict with the Scots. He was supported by Anarawd, King of Gwynedd. When the Danish attacks were renewed, his kingdom disintegrated.

Deira was again under Danish rulers, and the names of Siefred and Cnut were mentioned. It seems that Anglian leaders in the North looked to Alfred of Wessex. Eadwulf, the High Reeve of Bamburgh, was friendly with the great opponent of Danish domination. Bernicia was not subject to the 'Danelaw'. In the Anglo-Saxon Chronicle 'Northumbria' is still used as a general term for those north of a river Tyne, though there were marked differences. When Eadwulf, the High Reeve of Bamburgh, died in 913, he was succeeded by his son, Ealdred.

Apart from these references, the North receives little mention in the Chronicles. The Danes were occupied with attacks on Wessex, and were also penetrating far into the land of the Franks. From 894 they attacked Wessex again in force, and were *joined by great reinforcements both from East Anglia and Northumbria."* They built a fort at Benfleet, but while they were out on harrying raids under their leader Haesten, the fort was taken by the English. The host was defeated in battle on the Severn. Many were killed, but others were saved by flight.

"When they came to their fort and to their ships in Essex, the remainder gathered together a great host from East Anglia and Northumbria before winter: and placing their women, their ships and their property in safety in East Anglia, they marched without halt by day and night until they arrived at a deserted Roman site in Wirral, called Chester. The levies were unable to overtake them before they got inside that fort, but they besieged it some two days, and seized all the cattle in the vicinity, slaying all the men they could intercept outside the fort: they burnt up all the corn and with their horses ate all the neighbourhood bare."

This gives a dramatic picture of the methods and mobility of the Danes. It also illustrates their ability to use forts, and in particular to defend Chester. On the other hand, Alfred had reorganised his army so that it could be kept in the field all the year. The English also adopted a scorched earth policy, depriving the Danes of corn.

The host was forced to move into Wales, but *"They were unable to remain there because they had been deprived of both the cattle and the corn which had been plundered. Then again they moved from Wales with the plunder they had taken there, marching across Northumbria and East Anglia so that the levies were unable to get them until they reached Essex on an island called Mersea."* This was in 895, and they had a fort on the Lea. In 896, the English encamped near the fort to protect the gathering of the corn and to prevent the Danes from getting it. Alfred also trapped their ships on the river by a barrier, and they were forced to go to Bridgenorth on the Severn, where they built a fort. The women were in safety in East Anglia. *"Then the following summer, 897, the host dispersed some to East*

Anglia, some to Northumbria and those without stock got themselves ships there and sailed South oversea to the Seine." They reverted to raiding, but Alfred buil bigger ships to check them.

Alfred died in 899, and was succeeded by his son Edward. Aethelwold, a relative, was in rebellion, but escaped to Northumbria *"which received him as king and submitted to him."* Apparently, he attempted to abduct a lady who was under vows. Aethelwold now led the host against Wessex, and after severe fighting, in which Aethelwold was slain, Edward made peace in 906. His sister Aethelflede, the Lady of the Mercians, defeated the host at Tettenhall in 909. In 910 Edward sen levies and severely harried the host in the North, destroying both people and ever kind of cattle. After the host in Northumbria broke the truce (911) he intercepte them in their harrying and put them to flight, killing many.

Danish rulers in the North had joined the invaders who attacked the lands rule by Alfred. It seems that the lands in the North were not so rich, and had suffere plunder already. Halfdene had found them unprofitable. Northern Northumbria wa largely free of the Danes in respect of settlements, so was Scotland. Perhaps it wa partly a matter of communications since the Danes seem to have used rivers a grea deal – the Ouse and Trent, the Thames and Severn allowed deep penetration. Th coast of Deira was easy to raid, but the land itself was not so easy to penetrate an settle. The Danes seem to have preferred to settle in Yorkshire and southward Danish archaeological remains in Durham tend to come from the Hartlepool are These and the evidence of Scandinavian place-names are lacking i Northumberland. Settlement was enforced upon the Danes by circumstances. Th leaders were expected to provide not only plunder, in the form of gold and silver fc taking away, but also present needs had to be satisfied by gifts of horses, cattle an corn. These might come from robbery or tribute, but when such supplies were n available the Danes themselves were in dire peril. Murrain among cattle affecte them too, and shortage of food could be a serious problem. In 914 many Danes in raiding party died of hunger.

Alfred's method had been an acceptable compromise – defined areas were to b the 'Danelaw'. The boundary for a considerable period was the Roman road c Watling Street. Alfred's successors attempted the reconquest of the Danelaw b means of establishing 'burhs', or fortified towns, in reconquered areas. Thes became administrative centres and parts of the shire organisation. A number e these naturally had been used by the Danes as their strategic and fortified centre They were captured and refortified by Edwin. In 917 Edward held Towcester o Watling Street against a combined Danish attack, and then proceeded to captu their river base at Tempsford. After this the Danish Earls submitted to Edward, an by 918 he had established his authority over all England south of the Humber.

In the North further changes were taking place. In the early 10th centur

Scandinavians were crossing from Ireland and settling in the North West. Raiders also came from the same direction. This caused much concern to local noblemen and churchmen, some of whom moved away. This area is characterised by a hybrid culture as shown by place-names, and in particular by carved crosses. The Solway area had been invaded by Scots from Strathclyde. This was made possible by the disintegration of Northumbria under Danish attacks.

The English rulers at Bamburgh were quite unable to prevent the Scots taking over this area. In fact they fought in alliance with Constantine, King of the Scots, against a Viking Raegnald who defeated them at Corbridge. This was in 914. Raegnald in 918 joined other Danes in fighting the Scots *"so that they met on the banks of the Tyne in the land of the Southern Saxons."* The fighting was indecisive except that Raegnald stayed on, and divided the estates of St Cuthbert south of the Tyne. In 919, he made himself King of York. His success helped the infiltration of the Vikings from the West. The Anglo-Saxon Chronicle presents King Edward's progress northwards and the building of a fortress at Bakewell. In 920 *"Then the King of the Scots and the whole Scottish nation accepted him as 'father and lord': so also did Raegnald and the sons of Eadwulf and all the inhabitants of Northumbria, both English and Danish, Norwegians and others: together with the King of the Strathclyde Welsh and all his subjects."*

It was all too flattering and might seem the result of inevitable advance by Edward. In fact, it was rather different. The northern rulers, some upstarts and others having taken over territory recently, saw the advantage of some official recognition. Ealdred represented a line of Bernician aristocrats who were established at Bamburgh, and had resisted Scots, Danes and Norwegians alike. King Edward might be used as an ally, if necessary, against further Scandinavian attacks.

King Aethelstan (924–939), son of Edward, had been brought up in Mercia, and was acceptable there. He married his sister to Sitric, Raegnald's successor at York, and when he died, Aethelstan invaded Northumbria. Olaf, son of Sitric and Guthfrith, King of Dublin, were driven out. Guthfrith took refuge in Scotland. *"King Aethelstan annexed the Kingdom of Northumbria: he brought into submission all the kings in this island: first Hywel, King of the West Welsh and Constantine, Kings of Scots and Owain, King of Gwent and Ealdred, Ealdulfing (Eadwulf's son) from Bamburgh. They established a covenant of peace with pledges and oaths at a place called Eamont Bridge on July 12: they forbade all idolatrous practices and separated in concord."* (Anglo Saxon Chronicle, 926)

But it seems the Scots did not keep the agreement, and in 934 Aethelstan, with the help of the Welsh princes, again made war.

"In this year King Aethelstan invaded Scotland both with a land and naval force and harried much of the country." This provoked the organisation by Constantine, *"the grey haired warrior"*, of a great hostile coalition of his own men

with warriors from across the sea, led by Olaf, Guthfrithson, King of Dublin, and Olaf Sihtricson, Constantine's own son-in law. Constantine hoped to gain Bernicia, and the King of Dublin to recover York. The battle site of Brunanburh cannot be certainly identified. In this great struggle both sides suffered heavy losses, but Aethelstan gained the victory. The Anglo-Saxon Chronicle praises the event in a poem for the year 937, and it gives a good idea of the terminology and ideas of the time.

> *"Aethelstan is the 'lord of warriors, ring-giver of men'.*
> *With their hammered blades, the sons of Edward,*
> *Clove the shield wall and hacked the linden bucklers,*
> *As was instinctive to them, from their ancestry,*
> *To defend their land, their treasures and their homes,*
> *In frequent battle against each enemy."*

Those who were killed included five young kings, seven jarls (earls) and many seamen (term for sea-raiders).

Constantine lost his young son *"mangled by wounds, received in the fight."*

> *"The sorry Norsemen who escaped the spears,*
> *Set out upon the sea of Ding, making for Dublin,*
> *O'er deep waters, in ships with nailed sides,*
> *Ashamed and shameless back to Ireland."*

The final grim picture of the battlefield, almost in border ballad fashion, gives the aftermath of the struggle. It is not the scene of heroes, buried with gold, or ship in high heaped mounds, but the presence of the wolf and the raven. These were the signs of death, and here many had fallen.

Aethelstan returned south. An illuminated medieval manuscript shows him presenting a book to St Cuthbert's Church at Chester-le-Street. Information about this period comes from the 'Historia Regum' attributed to Symeon of Durham. Aethelstan gave books, treasures and estate – such gifts were the basis of the wealth and power of the later Bishopric.

Aethelstan died in 939, leaving a difficult task to his brother Edmund (339–946), who was only eighteen. There was Northumbrian revolt, supported by Archbishop Wulfstan of York. Olaf Guthfrithson and then Olaf Sihtricson were rulers in turn, but it was not till 945 that Edmund was able to drive them out. He also ravaged Strathclyde, but granted it to Malcolm, King of the Scots, in return for an alliance – *"on condition that he would be his fellow worker both by land and sea."* Edmund was murdered in 946, and Northumbria accepted first Olaf Sihtricson and then Eric, 'Blood-axe', as Kings. It was not until 954 that Eadred secured recognition after Oswulf, Earl of Bamburgh, betrayed Eric and he was killed at Stainmoor. It shows there were deep divisions between Angle, Dane and Norseman. The Earl of Bamburgh pursued his own policy, playing off the Kings of Wessex and the Scandinavian rulers of York. The English Kings from Wessex were not long lived, and Eadred died in 955. Edmund's sons were used in opposition to each other by factions of nobles. Eadwig died in 959, and Edgar attempted to re-assert his authority over all England. The Anglo-Saxon Chronicle gives very little information about this, but a great deal about the restoration of the monastery at Peterborough. In 966 it is recorded: *"In this year Thored, son of Gunner, ravaged Westmorland and in the same year Oslac became Earl of Northumbria."* In 973 there was a grand ceremonial coronation of Edgar at Bath. *"Soon after this the King led all his fleet to Chester and there six kings came to him to make their submission and pledged themselves to be his fellow workers by land and sea."* They included Welsh and Scottish Kings. It was to them probably not an act of submission but an alliance to protect the country against further Viking attacks. A poem in Edgar's honour mentions that:

"Then too the bold hearted Oslac was driven from the land,
Over the tossing waves where the gannet bathes."

Northumbria was divided with a separate earl for Deira. The pattern of growth was of mighty ealdormen, accepting the King nominally. Regional differences had to be accepted with different laws and customs. This applied to the Northern Anglian areas as well as the Danish. This partly explains why another Scandinavian invasion in the reign of Ethelred II (978–1016) was successful.

The Scandinavian attacks had serious effects upon the Church in the North and though Christianity was not extinguished, it suffered severe setbacks from the pagans. St Cuthbert's relics left Lindisfarne (c.875), reposing at Chester-le-Street for a century, and finally reaching Durham (c.990). This became the ecclesiastical centre. The bishopric and community of Hexham had almost ceased to exist. Information from Durham indicates that the clergy were married men, living in their own houses, but maintaining a monastic type of service in the Church at Durham. There grew up a school for the education of clerics. Attempts to make Durham into a more regular monastic community failed.

During the reign of Edgar, under the influence of Archbishop Dunstan, a great deal was done to repair the damages of the Danish raids. Northumbria had lost its superiority in scholarship. Oswald, Bishop of Worcester, combined this see with York (972–992). Between 940 and the Norman Conquest some 60 monastic houses were founded or revived. But English monasteries retained a good deal more

73

contact with the world than was usual, and a number of monks became Bishops. Archbishop Dunstan was a monk statesman and scholar.

Edgar the Peaceful died in 875, and after a short reign his elder son Edward was murdered and replaced by Ethelred, who was aged 13. He seems to have been cursed by the fact that his reign began with murder. His name meant 'good counsel', but his nickname 'Unraed' means just the opposite. 'Unready' is not a fair interpretation, Ethelred was more unfortunate in that Scandinavian attacks were renewed on a large scale. The land was much divided, and the navy was not now adequate. The Vikings had established large bases on the continent – large enough for 3,000 men and almost impregnable. They had leaders like Olaf Trggvason, later King of Norway, who came in the raid of 991, and celebrated in the 325 verses of the'The Battle of Maldon', the fullest and most authoritative account of what took place. Earl Brihtnoth is the hero of the saga:

Then Bryhtnoth dressed his band of warriors,
from horseback taught each man his task,
where he should stand, how keep his station.
He bade them brace their linden-boards aright,
fast in finger-grip, and to fear not.
Then when his folk was fairly ranked
Bryhtnoth alighted where he loved best to be
and held most at heart - among hearth-companions.

Earl Bryhtnoth receives a messenger from the raiders:

'The swift-striking seafarers send to me thee,
bid me say that thou send for thy safety
rings, bracelets. Better for you
that you stay straightaway our onslaught with tribute
than that we should share bitter strife.
We need not meet if you can meet our needs:
for a gold tribute a truce is struck.

Art captain here: if thou tak'st this course,
art willing to pay thy people's ransom,
wilt render to Vikings what they think right,
buying our peace at our price,
we shall with that tribute turn back to ship,
fare out on the flood, and hold you as friends.'

It seems the seamen preferred this, but Brihtnoth declared himself faithful to King Ethelred:

'Hearest 'ou, seaman, what this folk sayeth?
Spears shall be all the tribute they send you,
viper-stained spears and the swords of forebears,
such a haul of harness as shall hardly profit you.

Spokesman for scavengers, go speak this back again,
bear your tribe a bitterer tale:
that there stands here 'mid his men not the meanest of Earls,
pledged to fight in this land's defence,
the land of Aethelred, my liege lord,
its soil, its folk. In this fight the heathen
shall fall. It would be a shame for your trouble
if you should with our silver away to ship
without fight offered. It is a fair step hither:
you have come a long way into our land.

But English silver is not so softly won:
first iron and edge shall make arbitrement,
harsh war-trial, ere we yield tribute.'

(taken from "The Earliest English Poems' trans. by Michael Alexander. Penguin.)

They fought and the heroic earl fell in battle, but not all Ethelred's earldormen were like Brihtnoth and were ready to negotiate with the raiders. The King himself was not averse to this, and until 1006 immerse sums of money were paid to the enemy in the form of 'Dane-geld'. An attempt to resist was made, but after this further payments followed. The Anglo-Saxon Chronicler is critical of Ethelred, but there is something to be said for this policy. Resistance was difficult to organise and expensive. The Danes had a superior fleet and could move quickly to attack, and then depart elsewhere. The English king could waste his time trying to catch them. Danish settlers and others were ready to co-operate with the invaders. On the other hand, some Danes were ready to co-operate and Thorkell the Tall, one of their leaders, took the service of King Ethelred.

In 1013 King Sweyn of Denmark himself came over, determined on the conquest of England. His success was rapid, and when Thorkell joined him, Ethelred had to seek refuge in Normandy. Sweyn died in 1015; he was then king of all England, but his son, Cnut, did not immediately resume the responsibility.

At this stage it is necessary to refer to local matters. Ethelred had attempted to strengthen his position by marriage. He, himself, had married Emma of Normandy. In the North, he can have had little influence, and Waltheof, who was Earl of Bamburgh from 975 to 1006, only once attended Court to pay his respects. When he died Ethelred made Waltheof's son, Utred, ruler of a united Deira and Bernicia. He married Ethelred's daughter, and this extended power was made possible by the assassination in 1006 of earldorman Aelfhelm by Eadric Streona, 'the Acquisitor', and adviser of the King. Eadric became earldorman of Mercia, and also married a daughter of Ethelred. Utred seems to have made peace with Sweyn in 1013, and when Ethelred returned he was deprived of York.

In 1015 Eadric Streona assassinated Morcar and Sigeferth, leading thegns in the Seven Boroughs. Edmund Ironside, Ethelred's son, married Sigeferth's widow, and took over his estates in spite of his father. Edmund restored York to Utred, thereupon Eadric gave his support to Cnut, the Danish claimant. Cnut married Aelfgifu, the widow of Aelfhelm, who had been killed by Eadric in 1006. Eadric's support gave Cnut an advantage over Edmund Ironside, who claimed the throne on the death of his father in 1016. Utred of Northumbria, who supported Edmund, was killed in 1016 through the treachery of Eadric. Edmund himself was defeated and died shortly afterwards.

Cnut was now unchallenged as king, and was accepted by the West Saxons. The power-seeking Eadric was confirmed for a term in his earldom of Mercia. Thorkell became Earl of East Anglia and Eric of Norway was confirmed in possession of Northumbria. Bernicia remained under its own Earl. Despite his association with Aelfgifu, by whom he had two sons, Swein and Harold, Cnut married Emma, Ethelred's widow, to strengthen his position. Aelfgifu acted for him in Denmark. Cnut got rid of Eadric Streona on Christmas Day 1017. The Scots won a battle at Carham on Tweed, and Cnut had to lead an expedition in Scotland to compel their submission.

After this the country was comparatively peaceful. Cnut laid on taxes, but established a very efficient administration. The different 'laws' of different parts of the country were accepted though some general regulations were enforced. Cnut kept a strong fighting force and his kingdom was secure enough to allow him to visit Denmark in 1020 and Rome in 1027. Here he met Pope and Emperor, and was very conscious of his royal dignity. His earls were mostly Scandinavian. Godwin, who was not, was related to Cnut by marriage, and became Earl of Wessex. Siward of Northumbria, who lived till 1065, was Danish.

The Anglo-Saxon Chronicle has very little to report on Cnut's reign, perhaps because of the lack of exciting incident, showing the success of efficiency of the King. Ethelred's reign had been full of wars and trouble. This example may serve recording in 1012 the death of Archbishop Aelfheah. The Danes under Thorkell had enforced tribute from London, but Archbishop Aelfheah proved obstinate. Thorkel tried to control his men. *"Then on the Saturday the host became greatly incensed against the Bishop, because he was not willing to offer them any money and forbade any ransom to be given for him. Moreover they were very drunk for wine had been brought to them from the South. Then they took the Bishop and led him to their tribunal on Saturday evening (April 19) and pelted him to death with bones and heads of cattle and one of them smote him on the skull with the iron of an axe, so that with the blow he sank down and his holy blood fell upon the earth and his holy soul was sent forth to God's kingdom."*

Trouble returned with Cnut's death. He intended his son Harthacnut to succeed him in all his lands. But in England, Harold with the help of his mother, Aelfgifu, seized the treasury and had the support of Mercia and the North. Harthacnut was accepted in Norway. The sons of Emma, Cnut's second wife, went to see her at Winchester. One of them, Alfred, was put to death and the other, Edward, escaped back to Normandy.

Harold's reign, however, was short, and in 1040 he was succeeded by Harthacnut. He was ruthless and violent, and taxed the country heavily to build up a great navy. His reign, too, was very brief.

One version of the Anglo-Saxon Chronicle reports:

"1042. In this year Harthacnut died as he stood at his drink, and he suddenly fell to the ground with a horrible convulsion; and those who were near thereto took hold of him, but he never spoke again and passed away on the 8th of June."

Another adds; *"In many and various ways this was the most disastrous year: the weather was severe and the crops suffered: during the same year more cattle died than anyone remembered before, either by reason of diseases of various kinds or because of the inclement weather."*

Edward, commonly called 'the Confessor' became king. His first actions were far from saintly.

"Soon after the king had all the lands which his mother owned confiscated for his own use, and took from her all she possessed, an indescribable number of things of gold and silver, because she had been too tight-fisted for him."

Edward, aged about 40, had spent most of his time in Normandy. His kingdom was Anglo-Danish, and strong regional differences had been recognised by previous kings of England. Cnut accepted the former kingdoms as Earldoms, but he was capable of keeping them under control. Edward lacked the experience and ability. He tended to rely on Normans, such as Archbishop Robert, who were given important positions. This was resented by the great Earls – Godwine of Essex, Leofric of Mercia and Siward of Northumbria.

Godwine was ambitious, but Edward, who married Godwine's daughter, was not a saintly nonentity. He was hot tempered, loved hunting and had the greatest regard for the warrior king Olaf of Norway. Edward beat off Viking attacks and pursued his own foreign policy. His success helped him to reduce his army and navy. So far he had successfully opposed Godwine, who in 1051 was exiled. He had depended on Leofric and Siward, but in 1052, when Godwine returned with force, they were not inclined to civil war. Godwine was restored, but never able to dominate the King. He was succeeded as Earl of Wessex by his son, Harold, in 1053.

Earl Siward of Northumbria was a great fighter. He extended his power by slaying Eadulph and acquiring Bernicia. When Macbeth became ruler of Scotland by killing Duncan, Malcolm Canmore took refuge with Siward. Later Siward helped him to defeat the usurper and recover his throne.

"1054. This year Earl Siward marched with great host into Scotland and made great slaughter of Scots and put them to flight, but the King escaped. On his side fell many, both Danes and English, also his own son."

Another version: *"Earl Siward invaded Scotland with a great host both by land and sea and fought against the Scots. He put to flight their King Macbeth and slew the noblest in the land carrying off much plunder, such as none had previously gained. But his son, Osbern, and his sister's son, Siward, and numbers of his housecarles as well as those of the king were slain there on the festival of the Seven Sleepers (27 July)."*

"In the same year Osgod Capa (the Goggle-eyed) died in his bed" – an event so unusual that one would like to hear more about it.

When Earl Siward died *"To Tostig, son of Earl Godwine, the king gave the earldom."* This was in the year 1055. Tostig was a stern ruler, and determined to enforce order. In 1061 he was able to go with his wife to Rome at the same time as Ealdred received the pallium as Archbishop of York from the Pope. In 1063 we find him fighting for his brother, Harold, against the Welsh. The King Gruffudd was killed, and Harold, after receiving his severed head, sent it on to the King.

In 1065 there was a revolt against Tostig. *"Soon afterwards all the thanes of Yorkshire and Northumberland came together and outlawed their Earl Tostig, slew all his retainers whom they could catch, whether English or Dane, and seized his stock of weapons at York, and his gold and silver and all his treasures which they came to hear of anywhere there. They sent for Morcar, son of Earl Aelfgar, and chose him to be their Earl."*

Edwin of Mercia and Morcar of Northumbria (his brother) met Harold at Northampton with a request to accept Morcar in Tostig's place. *"While he was away the Northerners did much damage at Northampton: not only did they slay men and burn houses and corn, but carried off all the live-stock they could find amounting to many thousands. They took many hundreds of captives and carried them North with them, so that the shire and other neighbouring shires were for many years the poorer."*

Gryth, Harold's brother, was Earl of East Anglia, and the action of the northerners was intended to apply pressure on Harold and the King. *"All the men of Tostig's earldom were unanimous in repudiating him and all with him who had promoted injustice because he robbed God first and then despoiled of life and land all those over whom he could tyrannize."* Tostig was forced to retire with his wife to Flanders. He was to return in 1066.

The house of Godwine was now balanced by the house of Leofric, two brothers holding Mercia and Northumbria. At this time, with the King ageing and childless, the most important problem was the succession.

England was nominally under one ruler, but the King had very little influence in the North. In mentioning the problem of the succession briefly, it will be seen that there was no divine right or primogeniture. The approbation of or election by the Witan was all important. William of Normandy's claim was slender, and Harold Godwinson by marriage was also related to the King. It seems too that Edward, at the end, accepted Harold, but it is difficult to see the real situation on account of Norman propaganda. When Edward died on January 5, 1066, Harold was readily accepted as his natural successor.

> *"Yet did the wise King entrust his kingdom*
> *To a man of high rank, to Harold himself,*
> *The noble earl, who ever*
> *Faithfully obeyed his noble lord*
> *In words and deeds, neglecting nothing,*
> *Whereof the national king stood in need."*

In April Tostig returned to cause trouble. He raided the south coast, and did much damage till he was driven away. Then he attacked Lindsey, but was again forced to leave, and finally sailed to Scotland. Here he was joined by Harold Hardrada, King of Norway, who had a great reputation as a fighter and became the hero of a saga.

This man was one rival claimant to Harold Godwinson and the other was William, commonly called 'The Bastard', of Normandy, who was second cousin to the late King Edward. William always argued that Edward had promised the throne to him, and that Harold in 1064 had solemnly promised to support him. The Normans were of Scandinavian descent, and William had the reputation of a hard fighter. So Harold of England had two powerful rivals and strangely enough, fate, fortune, chance or, more prosaically, the weather was to have the greatest effect on the lives of the men involved, and the destiny of England.

If Hardrada won, England would be linked to Scandinavia. William's victory would connect England closely with the continent and the reforming Roman

Church. If Harold survived both challenges, he would be the hero of the whole nation and Saxon vitality would have immense opportunities for development.

Harold kept his ships and levies together for the whole summer, waiting. Early in September, when they had been disbanded, Harold Hardrada first arrived, making a common cause with Tostig.

"Then while the ships were in port, King Harald from Norway came unexpectedly North into the Tyne with a great pirate host – it was anything but small for it numbered about 300 ships or more – and the Earl Tostig joined him as they had previously agreed, with all the host he had been able to master. They sailed together with their combined troops along the Ouse up towards York. King Harold, to the South, was informed when he came ashore that King Harald and Earl Tostig had landed near York. Thereupon he marched northwards day and night as quickly as he could assemble his levies: but before King Harold could arrive, Earl Edwin and Earl Morcar had gathered as great a force as they could from their earldom and fought that host and made great slaughter of them, but a great number of the English were either slain or drowned or driven in flight and the Norwegians had possession of the place of slaughter."

This was the Battle of Fulford, and the Norwegians were perhaps over-confident with success. They were surprised by the arrival of Harold, who caught them some miles from their naval base at Riccall. Snorri's 'Saga' indicates they were not properly armed. To Tostig, Harold offered a share of his kingdom, to Hardrada seven feet of land for a grave. The great battle was fought at Stamford Bridge and Harold of England was completely victorious.

"There were slain Harald the Fairhaired and Earl Tostig and the remaining Norwegians were put to flight, while the English fiercely assailed their rear until some of them reached their ships: some were drowned, others burnt to death and thus perished in various ways so that there were few survivors." These having made promises of peace to the English King, sailed home in 24 ships. Harold had settled the menace of Scandinavian raids, but news came that William of Normandy had landed on September 28.

Harold returned South, perhaps far too hurriedly. He left himself no time to gather an army or wait for levies from further North. He rushed to battle, taking local levies, some not properly trained. Perhaps he was over-confident and underestimated his enemy. He may have been misinformed as to William's strength. William's landing was methodical, and a castle had been constructed as a defensive base.

The Anglo-Saxon Chronicle mentions the Norman invasion very briefly. *"Then Duke William sailed from Normandy into Pevensey, on the eve of Michaelmas (September 28). As soon as his men were fit for service, they constructed a castle at Hastings. When King Harold was informed of this, he gathered together a great* host and came to oppose him at the grey apple-tree, and William came upon him unexpectedly before his army was set in order. Nevertheless the King fought against him most resolutely with those men who wished to stand by him and there was great slaughter on both sides. King Harold was slain and Leofwine, his brother, and Earl Gurth, his brother, and many good men. The French had possession of the place of slaughter, as God granted them, because of the nation's sins."

Prince Edgar, Earl Edwin of Mercia and Earl Morcar of Northumbria submitted to William. They gave hostages to him and swore oaths of fealty. William promised to be a good lord and accept the best practice of his predecessors. He was crowned at Westminster on Christmas Day 1066. An incident showed the difficulties of understanding. 'The acclamation' of the King, a great shout, was mistaken by the Normans for the beginning of a riot. The English were to find that they had acquired an efficient, but harsh, ruler. The signs of the new order were the castle, as constructed at Pevensey; the abbey, as on the site of the battle; and heavy taxation. The invaders, who were Bretons as well as Normans, were to provide a ruling aristocracy.

England was turned from connections with Scandinavia to direct relationship with France. This tended to increase the importance of the South of England as compared with the North. The North had suffered terribly from Danish attacks and was to suffer more from the ravages of the Normans.

Part of Rothbury cross.

81

SOME CONCLUSIONS

"In the Anglo-Saxon period were laid the foundations of the English language, of English literature, art, government and administration, of English ecclesiastical organization and of English medieval piety."

The necessity of paying Danegeld had led to rapid financial developments – to quick assessments of taxation and to the minting of acceptable currency. The royal writ was a ready method of justice and administration. The shire and hundred organisations were already established. There was the accepted custom of consultation by the King and the validity of existing chapters was accepted. Certain regulations were extended to the entire kingdom.

"We do not know how Northumbria was divided among its earldormen in its independent days. When it became part of the kingdom of England it was sometimes under a single earldorman, whereas sometimes Yorkshire was treated as a separate area."

There was also the mixture of Danish elements, and although Bernicia did not receive many Danish settlers, there were Earls of Danish blood. This helped to make the North a violent and lawless area, remote from the King's authority.

There was a particularly violent and lasting feud, which seemed to have persisted from the time when Ethelred II united the earldormanry of Bernicia with that of Deira under the authority of Earl Uhtred of Bamburgh. Uhtred was the son of Earl Waltheof the Elder and married Elfgiva, the King's daughter.

He seems to have aroused a good deal of hate, and in 1016 *"prince Edmund rode to Northumbria to Earl Uhtred."* Instead of opposing Cnut they harried Mercia. However, Uhtred was forced to submit to Cnut and give hostages at York. But here as he advanced to do homage, he was slain by his enemy Thurband. Aldred, Uhtred's son, in due course, avenged his father by killing Thurband. The feud was handed on to Thurband's son, Carl, but some attempt at reconciliation was made by the mediation of friends. Carl and Aldred became friends and planned to go to Rome on a pilgrimage. They were hindered by a storm and stayed at Carl's house at Rise. It seems that something stirred up the feud, and Carl killed Aldred in Rise-wood.

This is the period of Macbeth in Scotland, and Siward, Earl of Northumbria helped to bring about his downfall. Siward's son, Waltheof, inherited the feud through his mother Elfrida, Aldred's daughter, and in 1073, when he became Earl he avenged his grandfather's death. As Carl's sons and grandsons were feasting at Settrington they were wiped out with the exception of one who was spared for his gentle disposition. Another was fortunately absent from the feast.

In the 11th century there was a great deal of lawlessness. Theft, violence and murder were common offences. Attempts were made by lawgivers to persuade the offended family to accept compensation, rather than continue a feud. In order to check cattle stealing, it was important to get sales witnessed. *"It was said, of Northumbria in the mid eleventh century, that parties of 20 or 30 men could scarcely travel without being killed or robbed by the multitude of robbers lying in wait."*

The Laws of Northumbria have not survived, except for some relating to Northern priests. These are of interest as showing the various fines that could be imposed on priests for neglect of duty or for deliberate offences. It seems to have been quite normal for the priest to be married. This was not acceptable in the reformed Church of Norman times. Since the Kings of England, from the beginning of the 10th century onwards, attempted to extend regulations to all parts of the country, these can be used to provide information about Northern parts of the country. Here is a measure about the investigation of cattle:

"Nevertheless this measure is to be common to all the nation, whether Englishmen, Danes or Britons, in every province of my dominion, to the end that poor men and rich may possess what they rightly acquire, and a thief may not know where to dispose of stolen goods, although he steal anything and against their will they be so guarded against, that few of them shall escape." (The Laws of Edgar)

Although there were local laws and customs that were accepted, certain measures extended to the whole country as, for example, the organisation of courts.

For the purpose of administering justice, the hundred court met monthly under the reeve; borough courts met three times a year and shire courts twice a year. The latter, under the presidency of both Bishop and Earldorman, was to deal with more serious offences. Certain causes were reserved to the King's court. The local courts could deal with all customary law. Procedure in court involved a strict and rather elaborate ritual. The accuser had to back his oath of accusation by a number of compurgators or oath-helpers. If the accused could deny the charge with the requisite number of oath-helpers the case was dismissed. If he were unable to do this, he went to the ordeal.

The ordeal was a method of trial and not a form of punishment. It was regarded as the judgement of God. The Church took control of the proceedings and the ordeal was preceded by a three days' fast. Mass was celebrated, during which the accused was called upon to confess his guilt.

For the ordeal by water, he was give holy water to drink, and then he was thrown into a pool of water. If he sank he was innocent and had to be rapidly recovered. If he floated he was guilty, because the water refused to receive him. The ordeal by fire involved the carrying of a piece of hot iron for a distance of nine feet, and the ordeal by hot water imposed the task of recovering a stone from boiling water, wrist-deep. The three-fold ordeal meant elbow depth of water or increased weight of hot iron. The wound was bandaged for three days, and if it healed without festering the accused was clear. The accused could choose the form of his ordeal. For an accused cleric, the ordeal was to swallow consecrated bread, while saying a prayer to the effect that it might choke him if he spoke falsely.

If the accused were found guilty the penalty prescribed by law would follow. For 'bootless' offences (i.e. where no payment could be made) it was death by hanging or stoning. But there might well be a fine instead; for certain types of murder it was possible to pay compensation called wergild. The amount depended on the rank of the person and the place where the killing took place. The alternative for inability to pay could be enslavement for life. The value of a man's 'peace' also depended on his rank, the most expensive peace being that of the King.

The main divisions of free society apart from the clergy, were the gesiths (later thegns) and churls. The wergild of the nobleman was six times that of the churl except in Kent: the amounts were 1200 shillings and 200 shillings, respectively. A noble was expected to have five hides of land – this was the basis of the provision for a soldier in the army. His main duties were military service, construction of fortifications and the repair of bridges. (A hide has been roughly estimated at 120 acres.)

"If a churl prospered, so that he had five hides of land of his own, a church and a kitchen, a bellhouse and a castle gate, a seat and a special office in the king's hall, then he was henceforth worthy of the status of a thane."

The churl's normal holding was one hide, enough for one household and enough for a full plough team and plough of his own. He might own more than this and was essentially free.

There were estate peasants who were given small holdings, stock and tools by the lord. In return they had to do fixed labour services weekly, pay small rents in kind and take part in 'boonwork' at certain times. The lord had his own specialist workmen as well.

The English economy was based mainly on agriculture and the village. There were, of course, isolated farmsteads as well as the collective village holdings. A good deal of land was obtained by bringing into cultivation both waste and woodland. (Place-names like Nunriding and Newton Underwood.) In the less fertile areas, especially in the North, there was extensive cultivation, so that the plough was taken over a much wider area in course of time. There is evidence of several open fields (i.e. more than two) in a number of Northumberland Villages *(c.j. Agricultural History Review)*.

The general pattern, however, was that while one field was sown in winter with corn, another was cultivated and sown in spring, while the third lay fallow. In each field each tenant had a fixed number of scattered strips. These units were of a day's ploughing commonly called the 'acre', though the area in fact varied. This ploughing pattern is the origin of much ridge and furrow – it was done by the eight-ox plough and required wide headlands for turning. The main crops were wheat for bread and barley for brewing, with some rye, beans and peas. (Our well-known vegetables were missing.) The villagers had shares in the meadows and common pastures. The animals were much reduced by slaughter before winter came with its shortage of fodder. Their flesh was salted – salt, a product that had to be obtained from outside the village. The salt pedlar with his cart was an annual visitor.

Food supplies were not at all certain. In addition to natural disasters, there were dangers of robbery and Danish attacks must have reduced many to misery. Slavery could be the end – either the result of destitution or through captivity. Prisoners, who could not be redeemed, might well be sold into slavery.

The slave had no rights and his worth was assessed at 20 shillings, paid to his master, if he were killed. The Church, often without success, attempted to prevent harsh treatment. The ploughman in Aelfric's Colloquy was not free. He says of his work:

"I go out at dawn driving the oxen to the field and yoke them to the plough. It is never so harsh a winter that I dare lurk at home for fear of my master, but when the oxen have been yoked and the ploughshare and coulter fastened to the plough, I must plough each day a full acre or more... I must fill the oxen's manger with hay and water them and clear out the dung."

The ploughboy, his assistant, had a hard life too.

A runaway slave could be stoned to death, and some might attempt to join the Vikings. Many slaves were the descendants of the Britons; others were captured in the wars. They might buy their freedom or be released by their owners. The ceremony often took place in church.

Here is quoted a document of manumission (freeing slaves) from County Durham in the 10th century:

"(Geatfleda) has given freedom for the love of God and for the need of her soul: namely Ecceard the smith and Aelfstan, his wife, and all their offspring, born and unborn, and Arcil and Cole and Ecgferth and Ealdun's daughter and all those whose heads she took for their food (i.e. accepted as slaves to save them from starvation) *in the evil days. Whatsoever perverts this and robs her soul of this, may God Almighty rob him of his life and of the heavenly kingdom, and may he be accursed dead and alive ever into eternity. And also, she has freed the men whom he begged from Cwaespatric namely Aelfwold and Collrand and Aelfsige and his son Gamal, Ethelred Tredewude and his stepson Uhtred, Aculf and Thurkil and Aelfsige. Whoever deprives them of this, may God Almighty and St Cuthbert be angry with him."*

Another piece of evidence about the 'evil days' is the Hexham hoard.

"A valuable discovery was made on the 15th of October, 1832, while digging a

grave on the western side of the churchyard, when a bronze vessel, shaped like a bucket; was met with. Its dimensions are ten and three quarter inches high [27cm], nine and three quarter inches [25cm] in diamteter at the bottom and seven and a quarter inches [18cm] at the top. The vessel was filled with bronze coins known as stycas, struck in the reigns of Eanred, Ethelred, Redulf, Osbercht and Aella, Kings of Northumbria, and during the pontificates of Eanbald, Wigmund and Wulfere, Archbishops of York. The coins were about 9000 in number and though they were at first dispersed through many hands, many have found their way to the British Museum, while the Society of Antiquaries possesses about a hundred well-selected specimens. It has been conjectured that the coins had been hidden during Halfdene's invasion in the year 875."   N.C.H. Hexham.

The stycas were typical northern coinage before the penny, and the hoard represents a considerable fortune. Those who did the hiding never returned.

From Hexham, too, comes a fine embossed silver plate with the representation of a saint upon it and part of a leather scabbard of the Viking period. The Church had suffered a great deal since Wilfrid's time, and when the Normans came the monastic sites of the North were derelict for the most part.

In the Anglo-Saxon period the foundations of our society were laid and much of modern English life and language have grown from Saxon roots. Our government laws, parliament, our system of shires, society and literature are basically Anglo-Saxon. Place-names date from this period and many limits of villages and estates were land cut. Our parishes and ecclesiastical organisations come from this time. Artistic influences have persisted and their dating of historical events. In these processes, the North East played no small part. The Golden Age of Northumbria is not just the reflected glory of a sunset, but a stimulus to further enlightenment.

Cross-slab at Jarrow.

Books and References

Anglo Saxon Chronicle. D. Whitlock. Eyre & Spottiswoode. 1961.

Anglo Saxon Chronicle. G.N. Garmonsway. Everyman Edition. Dent. 1960.

Bede's Ecclesiastical History. ed. L. Shirley Price. Penguin. 1955.

Backhouse, J. The Lindisfarne Gospels. Phaidon.

Bailey, R. Viking Age Sculpture in Northern England.

Bailey, R., Cambridge, E., Briggs, D. Dowsing and Church Archaeology.

Battiscombe, C.F. Relics of St. Cuthbert.

Beowulf. trans. by D. Wright. Penguin. 1957.

Bronsted, J. The Vikings. Penguin.

Brooke, C. Saxon and Norman Kings. Batsford. 1963.

Bruce Mitford, R.L.S. Sutton Hoo Burial Book. B.M. 1968.

Cameron, K. English Place Names. Batsford. 1961.

Campbell, J. Anglo Saxons. Phaidon. 1982.

Collingwood, W.G. Northumbrian Crosses in the Norman Age.

Cramp, R. Monastic Sites in D.W. Wilson's Archaeology.

Ekwall, E. Oxford Dictionary of Place Names. O.U.P.

Farmer, D.H. Oxford Dictionary of Saints. O.U.P.

Higham, N. The Kingdom of Northumbria. A. Sutton. 1993.

HMSO. Map of Dark Age Britain.

Hodgkin, R. History of the Anglo Saxons. O.U.P. 1952.

Hope Taylor, B. Yeavering. HMSO. 1977.

Hunter Blair, P. Introduction to Anglo Saxon England.

Hunter Blair, P. Northumbria in the Age of Bede. 1970.

Kirby, D.P. St. Wilfrid of Hexham. 1974.

Kirby, D.P. The Making of Early England. Batsford. 1967.

Marsden, J. Northanhymbre Saga. Kyle Cathie. 1992.

Mawer, H. Place Names in Northumberland and Durham. C.U.P. 1920.

Northumberland County History. Vol.3. Hexham.

Page, R.I. Life in Anglo Saxon England. Batsford. 1970.

Pevsner, N. Buildings of Durham, Cumbria and Northumberland.

St. Joseph, Dr. Monastic Sites From the Air. C.U.P.

Talbot Rice, D. The Dark Ages. Thames & Hudson.

Taylor, H.M. & J. Anglo Saxon Architecture. 3 vols. C.U.P. 1965.

Webb, J.F. Lives of the Saints. Penguin.

Welch, M. Anglo Saxon England. English Heritage. 1992.

Whitlock, D. Beginnings of English Society. Penguin. 1952.

Whitlock, D. English Historical Documents. Vol. 1. Eyre & Spottiswoode. 1968.

Wilson, D.M. Archaeology in Anglo Saxon England.

Wilson, D.M. Anglo Saxons. Penguin. 1971.

Important Dates

A.D.

410	Romans have left Britain. Barbarians attack Rome.
449	Saxon settlements – Hengist and Horsa.
463	Death of St Patrick, missionary to Ireland.
	Saxons are pagans.
520	Columba born in Ireland.
560	Columba brings Christianity to Iona.
597	Augustine from Rome converts Ethelbert of Kent.
603	Aethelfrith, who united Deira and Bernicia into Northumbria, defeats the King of the Scots.
616	Edwin, King of Northumbria, wages war and extends his power. Bretwalda – Lord of Britain.
627	Paulinus converts Edwin to Christianity.
632	Edwin killed in battle at Hadfield.
634	King Oswald defeats Cadwallon at Heavenfield.
635	Mission of St Aidan from Iona to Lindisfarne.
642	King Oswald killed in battle. Oswy King of Northumbria.
664	Synod of Whitby to settle religious differences between Roman and Celtic churches. Colman and others return to Ireland.
687	Death of St Cuthbert.
685–704	Aldfrith, King of Northumbria.
709	Death of Wilfrid.
729	Ceolwulf king.
735	Death of Bede. Forewarning of wrath to come.
737	Ceolwulf becomes a monk. Eadbert king and involved in wars with Mercia and the Picts.
782	Alcuin of York received by the Emperor Charlemagne.
793	Viking attacks on Lindisfarne: Raids, robberies and destruction of churches.
850	The Danes wintered in England. The English are divided and defeated.
877	Danes settle in Mercia and East Anglia.
878	King Alfred of Wessex defeats the Danes.
886	Alfred makes treaty with Guthrum, who becomes Christian and rules the Danelaw.
899	Death of Alfred.

Important Dates

A.D.

902–924	Edward the Elder recovers land to the Humber.
	Viking kings rule in York.
925–39	Aethelstan king of all England.
937	Great victory at Brunanburh.
959–75	Reign of Edgar the Peaceful.
978–1016	Ethelred king and Viking attacks renewed.
1016–35	Canute king of all England.
1042–66	Edward the Confessor king.
	Country divided into earldoms.
1055–65	Tostig was Earl of Northumbria.
1066	Death of Edward and a year of battles.

      (1) Northern Earls defeated by Harald Hardrada at Fulton.

      (2) Harold of England defeats Hardrada at Stamford Bridge.

      (3) William of Normandy defeats Harold of England at the Battle of Hastings.

Note:

The Dukes of Normandy were descended from Rollo, a Danish leader who conquered part of France.

By 1066 the Normans were French speaking.

So in Norman England the languages were Latin (the Church), French and English.

GLOSSARY

Apse - semicircular end of chapel.

Arcade - series of columns and arches.

Baluster - pillar, bellied in shape.

Bretwalda - Overlord of Britain.

Burgh - a fortified town.

Churl - Freemen of the 200 shillings class.

Danegeld - tax to pay to Danish raiders.

Danelaw - area under Danish laws.

Doom - law or judgement.

Dowsing - using metal rods to discover hidden features.

Ealdorman - a nobleman.

Frithstool - Bishop's throne, as at Hexham.

Hide - unit of land about 120 acres.

High Reeves - important officials.

Hogback - grave slab in the shape of a roof.

Host - name given to the Danish army.

Housecarles - special soldiers or bodyguard of Saxon king.

Hundred - a division of the shire or county.

Lintel - horizontal beam or stone above an opening.

Moot - assembly or meeting.

Oppidum - large fortified settlement. e.g. Yeavering Bell.

Porticus - chapel or subsidiary cell of a church.

Quoins - dressed stones at angles of buildings.

Raed - counsel or advice.

Rebate - recess cut in a wall to receive door or shutter.

Reeve - an official or agent. Shire-reeve = sheriff.

Thegns (or Thanes) - upper class landowners and military men.

Tonsure - shaving of the head, sign of the religious (monks).

Tympanun - recessed space bounded by the cornices of a pediment.

Witan - assembly of wise men; Council.

Wergild - blood price, compensation payment for murder.

BEDE MONASTERY MUSEUM

Jarrow Hall, Church Bank, Jarrow, Tyne & Wear, NE32 3DY
Tel: (091) 4892106 Fax: (091) 4282361

Built c. 1800, the Museum tells the story of the Anglo-Saxon and Medieval Monastery of St. Paul's Jarrow, home of the Venerable Bede (A.D. 673-735). Early stained glass, sculpture, monastery model, audio-visual, exhibitions, special events, craft shop, TIC, herb garden, cafe.
Small admission charge.
Open : Nov.-Mar. Tues. - Sat. 11.00-4.30, Sun. 2.30-5.30;
April-Oct. Tues. - Sat. 10.00-5.30, Sun. 2.30-5.30.
Closed Christmas and New Year.

ST. PAUL'S CHURCH & MONASTIC SITE

Church Bank, Jarrow, Tyne & Wear.
Tel: (091) 4897052

Anglo-Saxon chancel - continuous use for 1300 years.
Dedication stone 23 April AD 685.
Earliest Anglo-Saxon coloured glass.
Home of Venerable Bede.
Open: All year, Mon.-Sat. 10.00a.m.- 4.30p.m. Sun. 2.30p.m.-4.30p.m.

SAINT PAUL'S MONASTERY

Jarrow, Tyne & Wear.

Founded 682, home of the Venerable Bede, refounded 1075. Remains of cloister buildings. Part of Bede's church survived as a chancel of the Parish Church.

Open: Any reasonable time.

MUSEUM OF ANTIQUITIES

The University, Newcastle upon Tyne, Tyne & Wear, NE1 7RU
Tel: (091) 2227844 Fax: (091) 2611182
Prehistoric, Roman, Anglo-Saxon and Medieval collections chiefly from Northumberland. Models of Hadrian's Wall and Mithraeum.

Open : Monday to Saturday 10.00a.m. to 5.00p.m.

Also published by Sandhill Press

THE GREAT GUNMAKER : the life of Lord Armstrong
by David Dougan

A fascinating biography of William Armstrong, one of the nineteenth century's leading arms manufacturers.

Paperback. £5.95 ISBN 0946098 23 9

IN AND AROUND
ALNWICK...MORPETH...ROTHBURY...WARKWORTH
by Ian Smith

First in a new series in which Ian explores Northumberland's towns, villages and their rivers. Written in the author's inimitable style, the book also includes Ian's own line drawings and maps.

Paperback. £3.95 ISBN 0 946098 26 3

THE LAST YEARS OF A FRONTIER
By D.L.W. Tough

A history of the Borders during the turbulent times of Elizabeth I. Includes maps, illus. & material from original diaries, journals and manuscripts.

Hardback. £14.95 ISBN 0 946098 06 9

MEDIEVAL CASTLES, TOWERS, PELES & BASTLES
OF NORTHUMBERLAND
by T.H. Rowland

A reprint of this comprehensive guide to the many castles and Border strongholds which form part of Northumbria's rich, often troubled, history.

Paperback. £4.95 ISBN 0 946098 24 7

MYTH AND MAGIC OF NORTHUMBRIA
Retold by Sandhill Press

Stories traditionally told around firesides, ballads sung by minstrels, associated with well-known places in Northumbria, are retold here for your entertainment.

Paperback. £1.95 ISBN 0 946098 27 1